MW01198891

The Austro-Hungarian Forces in World War I (1)

1914–16

Peter Jung • Illustrated by Darko Pavlovic

Series editor Martin Windrow

First published in Great Britain in 2003 by Osprey Publishing
Elms Court, Chapel Way, Botley, Oxford OX2 9LP, United Kingdom
Email: **info@ospreypublishing.com**

A CIP catalogue record for this book is available from the British Library.

ISBN 1 84176 594 5

Editor: Martin Windrow
Design: Alan Hamp
Index by Alan Rutter
Map & chart by Darko Pavlovic
Originated by Electronic Page Company, Cwmbran, UK
Printed in China through World Print Ltd.

03 04 05 06 07   10 9 8 7 6 5 4 3 2 1

FOR A CATALOGUE OF ALL BOOKS PUBLISHED BY
OSPREY MILITARY AND AVIATION PLEASE CONTACT:

The Marketing Manager, Osprey Direct UK
PO Box 140, Wellingborough
Northants, NN8 2FA, United Kingdom
Email: **info@ospreydirect.co.uk**

The Marketing Manager, Osprey Direct USA
c/o MBI Publishing
729 Prospect Avenue, Osceola, WI 54020, USA
Email: **info@ospreydirectusa.com**

www.ospreypublishing.com

Dedication

Among the millions of soldiers from the nationalities of the
Austro-Hungarian monarchy, I would especially like to dedicate this
work to my grandfather, Franz Rotter of the
k.u.k. Eisenbahneregiment; also to Alois Rotter,
k.u.k. Ulanenregiment No.2 'Fürst Schwarzenberg', killed in action
in Serbia in 1915; to Friedrich Rotter, Maschinenbetriebsleiter II.Cl.
of the k.u.k. Kriegsmarine, who went down in SMS *Zenta* on 16
August 1914; to Anton Pelczar, Sapper, k.u.k. Sappeurspezialbataillon and in 1918 k.u.k. Sturmbataillon No.18; and finally
to Camillo Krätschmer of k.u.k. Fliegerkompanie 20 and later 43.
May they and all the other millions rest in peace.

Acknowledgments

During many years a number of people have kindly supported my
interest in the history and uniforms of World War I. My special
thanks go to Hofrat Dr Christoph Tepperberg, director of the
Kriegsarchiv, and to my colleagues Hofrat Dr Erich Hillbrand,
Hofrat Dr Peter Broucek, Oberrat Dr Robert Rill, Amtsdirektor Karl
Rossa and Amtsrat Otto Kellner. Further thanks for enormous
amounts of information over many conversations must be given to
the late Major Helmuth Krauhs, Oberst Anton Wagner and
Univ Prof Dr Franz Gall; to Dr Alessandro Geromella (Trieste),
Roland Sannicolo (Innsbruck), Dr Attila Bonhardt (Budapest),
Dr József Kelenik (Budapest), Univ Doz Dr Erwin Schmidl (Wien),
Dipl Ing Hermann Hinterstoisser (Salzburg), Mag Christian Ortner
(Wien), Mag Christoph Hatschek (Wien) and Mag Thomas Reichel
(Wien), Prof Dieter Winkler (Wien) and Amtsrat Roland Starrach
(Wien). Last but not least, special thanks to Dr Jerzy Gaul,
whose book on Polish Intelligence in World War I included most
informative photographic evidence for the uniforms of the
Polish legions.

Artist's Note

Readers may care to note that the original paintings from which the
colour plates in this book were prepared are available for private
sale. All reproduction copyright whatsoever is retained by the
Publishers. All enquiries should be addressed to:

Darko Pavlovic, Modecova 3, Zagreb, 10090, Croatia

The Publishers regret that they can enter into no correspondence
upon this matter.

THE AUSTRO-HUNGARIAN FORCES IN WORLD WAR I (1) 1914–16

INTRODUCTION

THE ARMED FORCES of the Austro-Hungarian monarchy are perhaps the most complicated single organisation to confront the researcher approaching the combatant powers of the Great War – a complexity born of both time and space. The forces of the Habsburg Empire were among the few in the Old World which could boast an impressively unbroken line of tradition over centuries of both victory and defeat. For hundreds of years they had formed the shield of Europe against the attacking Ottoman forces; and later, during the Napoleonic wars, the Austrians were present in nearly every major campaign against the French.

The army represented not only continuity over time, but also a unifying force over an enormously wide and diverse empire. From the mid-19th century the steadily increasing pressure of nationalist sentiments and aspirations initiated a gradual but constant process of imperial decline. In the Italian theatre of war the glorious victories won by Radetzky in 1848–49 were followed in 1859 by the decisive defeat at Solferino. In 1866 the Austrian Southern Army and the Navy were victorious in Italy, but the Northern Army suffered total defeat at Königgrätz (Sadowa), which entirely changed the political appearance of the Empire. In 1867 the Austro-Hungarian Dual Monarchy was established, giving more rights to the Hungarian provinces. From that time onward the political emphasis of the Empire shifted increasingly from a concentration on 'German' matters to a concern with Balkan and eastern affairs, and with the internal defence provoked by the growing nationalism of both the Slavic and the Italian communities within the imperial borders. Right up until 1918 the subversive activities of these groups were to prove a decisive factor, culminating in the downfall of the old Empire and its fragmentation into the new nations of Middle and Eastern Europe.

* * *

According to the military constitution of the Austro-Hungarian monarchy after 1867, the armed forces consisted of three autonomous organisations reflecting the constitutional background of the country. As common institutions the *kaiserliches und königliches gemeinsames Heer* ('Imperial and Royal Common Army') and *k.u.k. Kriegsmarine* ('Imperial and Royal Navy') represented the formal military power of the Dual Monarchy of Austria-Hungary. Distinct from the *k.u.k. Heer*, the *k.k. Landwehr* ('Imperial Royal Territorial Force') provided additional armed forces in the German-speaking half of the Empire; and the 'Royal Hungarian' *Honvéd (Magyar király Honvédség)* fulfilled the same role for

The Emperor Franz Joseph I (1830–1916); his reign, from 1848 until his death – four years longer than Queen Victoria's – was the major symbol of the unity and continuity of the Austro-Hungarian Dual Monarchy. The Archduke Friedrich represented him in the field until late 1916, when Franz Joseph died, to be succeeded by Karl I, who reclaimed supreme command of all armed forces for himself. (Kriegsarchiv)

the Hungarian regions. Officially the Common Army was the 'instrument of war' for military operations concerning the Empire as a whole, whereas the k.k. Landwehr and the k.u. Honvéd were initially intended solely as home defence troops; however, in the 20th century they had become integral parts of the field army.

To make it even more complicated, the administration was shared by three ministries. The *k.u.k. Kriegsministerium,* with a special Naval Section, was responsible for the Common Army, and ministries for 'home defence' for the Landwehr and the Honvéd existed simultaneously in Vienna and Budapest; naturally, each of the home defence and territorial forces and ministries used its own prinipal language. In the case of a large scale war these three organisations were to co-operate within the general concept of the *k.u.k. Wehrmacht* ('Imperial and Royal Armed Forces') – which, miraculously, did in practice work successfully for more than four years of war.

Compulsory national service had been introduced in 1867, and men were conscripted to serve both in the Common Army and in the Landwehr or Honvéd between the ages of 18 and 33 years. Behind the Landwehr and Honvéd stood the older men of the territorial Austrian *k.k. Landsturm* and the Hungarian *k.u. Landsturm (Magyar király Népfelkelo),* aged between 34 and 55 years. They were intended to provide replacement units for the first line forces when the latter were mobilised, but in reality the Landsturm formed its own field units – sometimes up to brigade size – and went on campaign with the rest of the army. Its fighting abilities improved noticeably during the years of the Great War.

In peacetime the k.u.k. Wehrmacht consisted of about 415,000 men, organised in 32 Common Army divisions, 16½ Landwehr and Honvéd divisions, 9 cavalry and 2 Honvéd cavalry divisions. This total could be increased upon mobilisation by 14 'march brigades' and 20 Landsturm brigades of reinforcements. According to official sources, the infantry in August 1914 comprised the impressive number of 929 battalions plus three volunteer battalions (Poles), to be followed shortly by 164 'march' battalions.

* * *

Formally, all the armed forces were directly under the command of the monarch, the Kaiser (Emperor) Franz Joseph I. Born in 1830, and thus 84 years old in 1914, in practice he was naturally unequal to the burdens of campaign. His designated heir, the Archduke Franz Ferdinand, had been appointed *Generalinspektor der gesamten bewaffneten Macht* ('Inspector General of all Armed Forces') as the first step towards his taking the supreme command when he succeeded Franz Joseph on the throne. This assured continuity was destroyed in a moment on 28 June 1914 during an official visit to Sarajevo in Bosnia, when a Serbian nationalist, Gavrilo Princip, assassinated both Archduke Franz Ferdinand and his wife Sophie von Hohenberg.

A month later the Old World – enmeshed in a net of defensive treaties – was on fire, dragged blindly into general warfare by a combination of militaristic ambitions and diplomatic helplessness. Franz Joseph I signed only four declarations of war – against Serbia (28 July), Russia (6 August), Japan (23 August) and Belgium (28 August). Nevertheless, Austria-Hungary received in all 13 declarations over the

The Archduke Franz Ferdinand and his wife the Duchess Sophie von Hohenberg, assassinated on 28 June 1914 at Sarajevo. The photographs were taken from the front page of the August edition of the Austrian Navy Leagues Journal *Die Flagge.* (Kriegsarchiv)

years until 1918: by Montenegro (on 5 August 1914), Great Britain and France (22 August 1914), Italy (23 May 1915), the USA (7 December 1917), and others from countries as irrelevant as Nicaragua, Panama and Cuba.

Over his reign of more than 60 years the old emperor had become something of a mystic figure, far above nationalistic or political disputes. From 1906 the professional head of military organisation and operational planning was the *Chef des Generalstabes für die gesamte bewaffnete Macht* ('Chief of the General Staff for the Armed Forces'), Franz Conrad von Hötzendorf, who still held this appointment in August 1914. The years before 1914 were dedicated to the intensive preparation of several contingency plans for operations against potential enemies, designated *Kriegsfall R* for Russia, 'B' for the Balkans, and (although the country was then officially part of the *Dreibund* or Triple Alliance), Plan 'I' against Italy. Combinations of these plans, such as synchronised operations against Russia and Serbia, or Serbia and Italy, were considered; but no 'wargames' were held to simulate the possibility of war in both the east and south-west, involving the Austro-Hungarian Empire on two separated fronts at the same time. Furthermore, although the wars of the early 20th century had been studied by the general staff, certain lessons of modern warfare – especially those demonstrated by the Boer and Russo-Japanese wars – were either neglected or disregarded by the responsible authorities. On the other hand, the strength of the Empire's forces was slightly overestimated. This, along with some confusion in the initial assembly of the troops against Serbia and Russia, led to a number of drawbacks and disasters within the first months of the war (see below).

Perhaps one of the greatest problems for the Common Army sprang from its national and ethnic diversity; it contained units drawn from eleven main nationalities – Austro-Germans, Hungarians, Italians, Romanians, Czechs, Slovaks, Poles, Ruthenians (Ukrainians), Slovenes, Serbs and Croats. Only 28 per cent of the personnel belonged to the dominant Austro-German population, followed by about 18 per cent Hungarians. The majority, 44 per cent, were Slavs; 8 per cent (including all groups from the northern, central and south-eastern regions) were Romanian, and about 2 per cent Italian. The movement for 'Panslavism' was already well entrenched, and in the south the Italian 'Irredentists' were increasingly demanding separation of their parts of the Empire and unification with the Kingdom of Italy. Perhaps surprisingly, in July-August

Staff officers in the Carpathian Mountains, winter 1914/15; note the tall, rigid cap. Apart from the variety of Army overcoats, some with fur collars, even civilian clothing might be worn. The wearing of two overcoats is documented in several photographs; see Plate D2. (Kriegsarchiv)

1914 general mobilisation was achieved with hardly any resistance from these elements; but problems were later to follow among the field armies.

ORGANISATION OF K.u.K. WEHRMACHT, AUGUST 1914–SPRING 1916

Following mobilisation, the Austro-Hungarian forces operated with six armies in the field, numbered 1st to 6th. While the k.u.k 1., 3., and 4. (later to be joined by the 2.) Armeen assembled in Galicia to face the Russians, the 5. and 6. formed the *Balkanstreitkräfte* or 'Balkan Command'.

In all, 18 army corps became operational. Of these, 16 were of peace-time origin; only XVII Korps (formed in August 1914), and the Armee-gruppe von Kummer (one cavalry division and two Landsturm infantry divisions) were wartime formations. Usually, each army corps comprised two to three infantry divisions, along with cavalry and technical formations under direct corps command; in reality the strength of the latter varied from time to time. A division usually had two infantry brigades, each consisting of two infantry regiments, totalling three or four battalions and a Feldjägerbataillon (rifle battalion); two squadrons of divisional cavalry; and one field artillery brigade with a mixture of guns and howitzers.

AUSTRO-HUNGARIAN ARMY CORPS DISTRICTS 1914

	ARMY CORPS BOUNDARIES
• Graz	ARMY CORPS HEADQUARTERS
	PROVINCE BOUNDARIES
	AUSTRIAN PART
	HUNGARIAN PART
	BOSNIA AND HERZEGOVINA

Additionally, further units up to divisional strength could be under direct command of an army.

These corps and army troops numbered in total: 50 infantry divisions (1.-48., plus 95. & 106. Landsturm Inf Divs), containing 93 infantry, 9 mountain and 44 field artillery brigades; and an additional 19 infantry, 5 mountain, 14 'march', and 5 Landsturm 'march' brigades. There were 11

Order of Battle, August 1914

k.u.k. 1. ARMEE
Commander: General der Kavallerie Viktor Dankl
I.KORPS (Krakau): 5.ID. (Olmütz), 46. LID. (Krakau):, Corps Troops
V. KORPS (Pozsony): 14.ID. (Pozsony), 33.ID. (Komárom), 37.HID. (Pozsony), Corps Troops
X.KORPS (Przemysl): 2.ID. (Jaroslau), 24 ID. (Przemysl), 45 LID (Przemysl), Corps Troops
Army Troops: 12.ID. (Krakau), 3.KD. (Wien), 9.KD (Lemberg) k.k.1.LstlBrig. (Wien), k.k.36.LstlBrig. (Leitmeritz), k.u.101.LstlBrig. (Budapest), k.k.110.LstlBrig. (Krakau), 1.MaBrig. (Krakau), 5.MaBrig. (Pozsony), 10.MaBrig.(Przemysl), Polnische Legion

k.u.k. Armeegruppe General der Infanterie Hermann Kövess von Kövoccháza (existing from 8 to 25 August 1914, then re-named k.u.k. 2. Armee with Kövess being the Commander of the XII. Korps)

k.u.k. 2. ARMEE
Commander: General der Kavallerie Eduard von Böhm-Ermolli
XII. KORPS (Nagyszeben): 16.ID. (Nagyszeben), 35.ID (Kolozsvár), 38.HID (Kolozsvár), Corps Troops
III. KORPS (Graz): 6.ID. (Graz), 28.ID (Laibach), 22.LID (Graz), Corps Troops
VII. KORPS (Temesvár): 17.ID. (Nagy-Várad), 34.ID (Temesvár), Corps Troops
IV. KORPS (Budapest): 31.ID. (Budapest), 32.ID (Budapest), Corps Troops
Army Troops: 11.ID. (Lemberg), 43.LID (Czernowitz), 20.HID (Nagy-Várad), 1.KD (Temesvár), 5. HKD (Budapest), 8.KD. (Stanislau): k.k.40.LstlBrig. (Brünn), k.u.102 LstlBrig. (Szegedin), k.u.103 LstlBrig. (Kolozsvár), k.k.105 LstlBrig. (Graz), 12.MaBrig. (Nagyszeben), MaFormationen der 20. HID., 38. HID.

k.u.k. 3. ARMEE
Commander: General der Kavallerie Rudolf Ritter von Brudermann
XI. KORPS (Lemberg): 30.ID. (Lemberg), k.k. 93.LstlBrig. (Lemberg), 11.MaBrig. (Lemberg), Corps Troops
XIV. KORPS (Innsbruck): 3.ID. (Linz), 8.ID (Bozen), 44.LID. (Innsbruck), 88.LSchBrig. (Bozen), Corps Troops
Army Troops: 41.HID. (Budapest), 23.HID.(Szegedin), 4.KD.(Lemberg), 2.KD (Pozsony), 11.HKD.(Debreczin), k.u.97.LstlBrig. (Kassa), k.k.108.LstlBrig. (Innsbruck), 3.MaBrig. (Graz), 14.MaBrig. (Innsbruck), MaFormationen der 41.HID., 4.MaBrig. (Budapest); MaFormationen of 23.HID were placed under command on 28 August

k.u.k. 4. ARMEE
Commander: General der Infanterie Moritz Ritter von Auffenberg
II. KORPS (Wien): 4.ID. (Br,nn), 25.ID (Wien), 13.LID.(Wien), Corps Troops

*VI. KORPS (Kassa):*15.ID. (Miskolcs), 27.ID (Kassa), 39.HID (Kassa), Corps Troops
IX. KORPS (Leitmeritz): 10.ID. (Josefstadt), 26.LID.(Leitmeritz), Corps Troops
XVII. KORPS - formed from 20 Aug. :19.ID. (Pilsen), 2.MaBrig. (Wien), 9.MaBrig. (Leitmeritz), Corps Troops
Army Troops: 6.KD. (Jaroslau), 10.KD (Budapest), 4.KBrig., 8.KBrig. 6.MaBrig. (Kassa)

k.u.k. Armeegruppe General der Kavallerie Heinrich Ritter Kummer von Falkenfeld
7.KD. (Krakau); k.k.95 LstID. (Prag), k.k.106 LstID.(Olmüz): Army group formations

k.u.k. Kommando der Balkanstreitkräfte (Balkan Forces Command)
Commander: Feldzeugmeister Oskar Potiorek

k.u.k. 5.ARMEE
Commander: General der Infanterie Liborius Ritter von Frank
VIII. KORPS (Prag): 9.ID. (Prag), 21. LID. (Prag), Corps Troops
*XIII. KORPS (Agram):*36.ID. (Agram), 42.HID. (Agram), 13.IBrig. (Esseg), Corps Troops
Army Troops: 11.GbBrig. (Tuzla), k.u.104. LstlBrig (Agram), 13.Mabrig. (Agram): MaFormationen der 42.HID.

k.u.k. 6.ARMEE
Commander: Feldzeugmeister Oskar Potiorek
XV. KORPS (Sarajevo): 1.ID. (Sarajevo), 48. ID.(Sarajevo), Corps Troops
XVI. KORPS (Ragusa): 18.ID. (Mostar), 47.ID.(Castelnuovo), 40.HID. (Budapest), k.u.109 LstlBrig., Corps Troops

Abbreviations
ID - Infanteriedivision (in 1914 the style was e.g.'Infanterie-*Truppen*-Division' for all types of division; since this was changed to the more international style during the war, the latter is used here to avoid confusion)
IBrig - Infanteriebrigade
KD - Kavalleriedivision
GbBrig - Gebirgsbrigade
LID - Landwehrinfanteriedivision
HID – Honvèdinfanteriedivision
HKD – Honvèdkavalleriedivision
LstID - Landsturminfanteriedivision
LstlBrig - Landsturminfanteriebrigade
MaFormationen - Marschformationen
MaBrig - Marschbrigade

Note
Throughout these tables German spelling is used for city names e.g. Wien/Vienna, Prag/Prague, Krakau/Kracow, etc.

Alpine troops being transferred by rail from Galicia to the new front opened up by Italy's declaration of war in May 1915. Note the snow goggles on their caps, and their long alpenstocks, here decorated with flowers and leaves. (Kriegsarchiv)

cavalry divisions (22 brigades), 17 k.k. Landsturm brigades, 9 k.u. Landsturm Etappen brigades, and 5 fortress artillery brigades.

By the spring of 1916 the organisation had grown to 26 corps plus 1 cavalry corps, numbering in total: 69 infantry divisions (including 111 infantry brigades, 4 half-brigades, 23 mountain brigades and 64 field artillery brigades); and additionally 13 infantry and 8 mountain brigades, 11 cavalry divisions (23 brigades), 3 cavalry brigades, 3 k.k. Landsturm brigades and 1 fortress artillery brigade.

In summer 1914 the artillery arm consisted of 483 batteries (field, mountain, heavy, and improvised guns and howitzers) with a total of 2,610 pieces. By 1916 the arm had grown to 804 batteries and 48 detachments with a total of 4,018 guns and howitzers.

Among the technical units the following selected facts are notable. Initially, 79 Sapper companies formed 14 sapper battalions. In spring 1916 the number of battalions was unchanged but they now comprised 100 companies, and an additional *Sappeurspezialbataillon* had been formed for gas warfare. The Pioneers had entered the war with 9 battalions comprising 43 companies, which had risen to 48 companies by 1916. The army telegraph service started with 11 detachments, 5 special telegraph detachments and 11 radio stations in 1914. By 1916 it had increased to 16 telegraph detachments, 6 special telegraph detachments, 30 field and 83 *Handradiostationen* (mobile field radio stations). Over this period the railway troops expanded from 28 companies to thirty-nine..

In 1914 army aviation comprised 15 *Fliegerkompanien*, 12 *Festungsballonabteilungen* (fortress balloon detachments) and one airship detachment; by spring 1916 it had expanded to 25 flying companies and 15 field balloon detachments.

Perhaps most impressive of all was the constant expansion of the automobile troops, which had entered the war with only 58 transport columns. In spring 1916 they numbered 191 lorry, 26 ambulance and 10 postal transport columns. Finally, the medical troops had nearly doubled their size during the first two years of the conflict.

PRINCIPAL OPERATIONS, AUGUST 1914–NOVEMBER 1916[1]

The assassination of Archduke Franz Ferdinand in Sarajevo on 28 June 1914 by a Serbian nationalist was followed by a month of hectic diplomatic activities. Partial mobilisation was ordered, preparatory

1 See also MAA 356 *Armies in the Balkans 1914–18*, MAA 364 *The Russian Army 1914–18*, and MAA 387 *The Italian Army of World War I*

to implementing Kriegsfall B (the contingency plan for war in the Balkans), involving three armies (k.u.k. 2., 5., and 6.) with eight corps, followed by the declaration of war against Serbia after an ultimatum had not been answered satisfactorily. Serbia was seen as a ringleader of the Pan-Slavic movement and her punishment had become a matter of political prestige. Only three days later, due to further political developments in Europe, the *Allgemeine Mobilisierung* or general mobilisation was ordered. In keeping with the structure of the army, the document signed by the emperor had to be delivered in three despatches of which two were in German and one in Hungarian.

The danger of a direct conflict with Russia, which supported Serbia, became evident at the beginning of August, and suddenly Kriegsfall B was considered less important. Under the contingency plan for war with Russsia, the k.u.k. 1., 4., and 3. Armeen were primarily scheduled for transport to the Galician front; and the 2. Armee, originally destined for operations against Serbia, had to be redirected to Galicia to support the right flank of the Austro-Hungarian forces.

In fact most of the 2. Armee were already en route to the Serbian border or had already arrived in their deployment zone. Needless to say, practically the entire railway system was already employed to capacity, and such changes of deployment were difficult to achieve. The transfer of the greater part of the 2. Armee from the Serbian border to Galicia was only possible from 18 August onwards, and its VII Korps and 29.Infanteriedivision remained on the Serbian front.

Ulans at their ease during the early weeks of the war in Galicia. They still wear full colour uniforms: light blue tunics with madder-red facings, and red breeches. The only concession to modern warfare is a light grey linen cover on the *czapka*. See Plate C2. (Kriegsarchiv)

1914

Meanwhile, operations against both Russia and Serbia had already begun. On 12 August the k.u.k. 5., and 6. Armeen opened the campaign against **Serbia**, forcing the River Drina. After some initial success the inferiority of the two armies fighting against three Serbian and the Montenegrin army became evident, and the troops were ordered back to their original positions.

In **Galicia**, linking up with the German 8th Army to their north, the k.u.k. 1., 4., and 3. Armeen were in line facing the Russians; the southern flank was given to the 2. Armee, whose late arrival proved decisive for the opening campaigns along this front. Since the German 8th Army had to face two Russian armies and was in permanent danger of being encircled, on 22 August the k.u.k. 1. Armee took the initiative by invading Russian territory in the direction of Lublin. A day later the Russian 4th Army was repelled in the battle of Krasnik. The same day, the k.u.k. 4. Armee also pressed forward from the area around Przemysl to the north. At the end of the consequent battle of Komarov (26 August – 1 September), the Russian 5th Army was forced to retreat and nearly encircled.

While the two Austrian armies were victorious in the north, on the southern flank the k.u.k. 3., and from the end of August the 2. Armeen, were confronted by superior Russian strength forcing an entry into eastern Galicia. An Austro-Hungarian counter-attack failed at Zlozow, forcing Gen von Hötzendorf to turn the main body of the k.u.k. 4. Armee in support of the right flank to stabilise the situation. Left alone, the k.u.k. 1. Armee came under pressure by much larger Russian forces and had to give way, constantly retreating south and thus leaving a gap between itself and the k.u.k. 4.Armee. Recognising this opportunity the Russians forced their way into this gap, putting the k.u.k. 4., 3., and 2. Armeen in danger of being encircled. The only possibility for the *Armeeoberkommando* (AOK – Army High Command) was to order a full retreat behind the River San; this was followed by the encirclement and first siege of the fortress of Przemysl by the Russians.

In early September 1914 a second offensive was launched against **Serbia**, but was soon brought to a halt by a Serbian thrust against Sarajevo which was only repelled after heavy fighting on 11 September.

Meanwhile the Russian high command had turned their primary attention against the Germans now isolated on the northern sector of the **Galician** front; but the Russians were heavily defeated in the battle of the Masurian Lakes (6-15 September).

The front line of the Austro-Hungarian forces along the Dunajec (k.u.k. 1., 4., and 3. Armeen) and in the Carpathian Mountains (2. Armee) had stabilized to a certain extent, but was still threatened by steadily growing Russian forces. As a gesture of support the Germans put their 9th Army into line to protect the k.u.k. 1. Armee's left flank. A combined offensive by these two armies reached the Weichsel-San line, relieving Przemysl for the first time. Superior Russian strength soon forced a halt and shortly afterwards a retreat to the old front line, leaving Przemysl besieged for a second time. Another danger arose for the k.u.k. 4. Armee, which had also advanced northwards; now the Russian 3rd Army endangered its eastern flank. The battle of Limanova-Lapanov (1-12 December) cleared the situation and forced the Russians to retreat, partly due to timely intervention by the k.u.k. 3. Armee. The severe winter conditions limited further operations by both sides.

They also had serious effects on the **Serbian** front, where the k.u.k. 5., and 6. Armeen advanced again during November and gained ground as far as Belgrade. However, while the 5. Armee was about to encircle the northern flank of the Serbian army, the latter counter-attacked against the 6. Armee, forcing the Austro-Hungarian troops into another retreat behind the River Save with heavy losses on both sides.

Arrival of a reinforcement column in the Carpathian front lines, early 1915; see Plate D3. Each regimental depot had a reserve battalion cadre, whose task was to send forward *'Marschkompanien'* or *'Marschbataillone'* of replacements to join the regiment on active service. These were sent at regular intervals – during the early part of the war a regiment might require one 'march battalion' each month. Before a major offensive 'march battalions' might be assembled into brigades. (Kriegsarchiv)

1915

During the winter of 1914/15 in **Galicia**, Gen von Hötzendorf planned the relief of Przemysl from the south by the k.u.k. 3. Armee and its right flank neighbour the smaller Army Group Pflanzer-Baltin, reinforced by the newly arrived German *Südarmee*. The offensive began on 23 January, but due to the severe weather conditions it gained practically no ground. Another attempt was made on 27 February by the 2. Armee, which was then deployed between the 3. and the German Südarmee; this too broke down in the face of heavy Russian resistance and appalling weather conditions. Left alone, Przemysl had to surrender on 23 March; 120,000 Austro-Hungarian defenders became prisoners of war. The night before the capitulation all remaining stores and artillery pieces were blown up, and even banknotes and stamps were burned in the banks and post offices.

On 20 March the Russians had launched an offensive against the k.u.k. 3. and 2. Armeen which pushed the front back behind the Carpathian Mountains. Another Russian attempt to break through into Hungary was halted at Easter 1915.

In all, the winter operations in the Carpathians had cost nearly 700,000 victims.

* * *

During the first months of the war, two Austro-Hungarian Common Army infantry regiments showed severe signs of instability. Both units – Infanterieregiment No.28 (Prague) and IR 36 (Jungbunzlau) – were drawn predominantly from Czech nationals. Several elements simply went over to the Russians, while others made little effort to defend their positions when attacked. As a result, in April and June 1915 these regiments were disbanded for 'cowardice in the face of the enemy'. IR 36 was deleted from all regimental lists, 'never to be raised again'. A *Marschbatallion* of IR 28, dominated by Bohemians of German background, was given the chance to redeem itself against the Italians on the Isonzo front. Here their behaviour was judged satisfactory, and in March 1916 the regiment would formally be re-raised; it continued fighting on the Italian front.

* * *

Both the German and Austro-Hungarian general staffs agreed to initiate decisive operations on the Eastern Front during 1915. On 2 May, with the German 11th Army in the lead, the offensive started with a break-through at Gorlice-Tarnów, supported by the Austro-Hungarian VI Korps with the Germans and on the right flank by the k.u.k. 4., and 3. Armeen. During the early stages the Russian 3rd Army launched a counter-offensive against the Austro-Hungarian southern flank with little success. Meanwhile, except for local counter-attacks by the Russians, the main offensive rushed forward like an avalanche. On 4 June Przemysl was retaken, and by 26 August Brest-Litowsk had been taken. The retreating Russians gave up nearly all Russo-Polish territory.

A trench south of Stratkov on the Galician front, 1915, manned by k.u.k. Infanterieregiment No.21 'Graf von Abensperg und Traun'. The sentry wears the standard field cap, greatcoat and puttees. (Kriegsarchiv)

A transport column with pack horses climbing an improvised mountain road in the Tyrol section of the Italian front, 1915. They wear the standard pike-grey woollen tunic with stand collar. Each regiment or independent battalion was supplied by its own pack trains, company carts and wagons; in total these carried 60 rounds of ammunition for every rifleman in the unit, plus pioneer tools, tailors', cobblers' and other repair equipment, baggage, field kitchens, medical supplies and unit paperwork. (Kriegsarchiv)

A further push east of Luck by the k.u.k. 4., and 1. Armeen was later halted by the Russians with considerable losses. In autumn 1915 the Galician front stabilized.

The Italian front

Meanwhile, on 23 May 1915, the Kingdom of Italy – neutral until now – had joined the Entente powers in the war against Germany and Austria-Hungary, opening a new front in the south-west running from the Swiss border through the high Alps and ending along the Isonzo river. The Italian aims were to conquer the southern part of the Tyrol on their left and/or to take Trieste and Istria on their right flank. The Italian advance opened during the Austro-German spring offensive in the East; the Austro-Hungarian general staff decided not to take troops from Galicia for the new front, but to build up the new line by shifting the k.u.k. 5. Armee from the Balkan theatre to the Isonzo. The defence of the mountainous regions – which had been heavily fortified since summer 1914 – was in the hands of the *Landesverteidigungskommando Tirol* ('Home Defence Command Tyrol') and the Armeegruppe Rohr along the Carinthian front.

The Italians attacked with great fury, both in the Alps and – as their main effort – with their 2nd and 3rd Armies along the Isonzo. So many battles would take place in this relatively limited region that historians would have to number them. The First to Fourth Battles of the Isonzo all took place in 1915, to be followed by the Fifth to Ninth in 1916.

The defence of the Italian front reunited most of the ethnic groups of the Empire for the last time; however, the AOK had learned from the episode of the two Czech regiments, and initiated some precautions against any repetition on this front. Ethnic Italians, especially from the southern part of the Tyrol, were posted to so-called 'South-West battalions' – even those from the Kaiserjäger regiments – and in theory these units served only on the Balkan (Romanian) or Eastern fronts.

Although permanently outnumbered, the Austro-Hungarian forces resisted even the heaviest Italian attacks, which in many cases came to bitter hand-to-hand fighting. In the high mountains of the Alps and Dolomites a new kind of warfare developed at enormous cost in lives and material. Logistics and all movement of heavy equipment presented tremendous problems especially during the winter, when avalanches also killed thousands of soldiers from both sides.

* * *

In autumn 1915 the final offensive against **Serbia** was launched, with considerable German help replacing the k.u.k. 5. Armee which had been shifted to the Isonzo front. Under the command of the German Generalfeldmarschall von Mackensen, Austro-Hungarian troops from Bosnia-Herzegovina and Dalmatia, together with the k.u.k. 3. Armee and

German 11th Army supported by two Bulgarian armies, entered Serbia on 5 October. By mid-December 1915 the country was conquered, but some 140,000 Serbian soldiers managed to retreat to the Adriatic coast, from where they were evacuated to the island of Corfu on ships provided by the Entente powers.

On the **Galician** front the winter of 1915/16 saw Russian activities against the k.u.k. 7. Armee (formed from the former Army Group Böhm-Ermolli) north of Czernowitz, but these met with little success.

The Tyrol, late 1915: an Alpine detachment preparing for a ski operation. All are dressed in the standard field cap and greatcoat, and most wear puttees. (Kriegsarchiv)

1916

In early January 1916 the k.u.k. 3. Armee took the offensive in the **Balkans**, invading Montenegro and reaching the capital Cetinje on the 14th. King Nicholas fled the country, and on 17 January the last groups of Montenegrin soldiers surrendered. The most impressive action in this campaign was the combined attack by land and naval forces to take Mount Lovcen overlooking the bay of Cattaro (Kotor), the southernmost Austro-Hungarian naval station.

The next objective was northern Albania, which was invaded by the XIX Korps supported by the VIII Korps. The Italians had invaded southern Albania in 1915, so this campaign was launched to prevent a possible further Italian advance. In northern Albania the Austro-Hungarian forces received a warm welcome from many of the population. On 9 February they reached the capital, Tirana; the port of Durazzo was fiercely defended by the Italians, but was taken on 26 February.

Clearly a posed photograph, but interesting in that it was taken in the highest trench of World War I – on Mount Ortler, about 12,700 feet (3,900m) above sea level. (Kriegsarchiv)

In April 1916 central Albania was occupied, and a defensive line along the Vojussa river was established by Austro-Hungarian battalions supported by local volunteers of the Albanian Legion.

With the situation stabilised in the Balkans, the AOK initiated a counter-offensive against **Italy** from

the southern Tirol (known as the *'Südtiroloffensive'* in Austria and the *'Strafexpedition'* in Italy). The aim was to overrun the Venetian plain and cut off the 2nd, 3rd and 4th Italian Armies. The offensive was planned to open in March, but due to the weather conditions it had to be postponed until 15 May.

Winter 1915/16 and early spring 1916 had seen fierce fighting in the mountains; this sometimes involved tunnelling under the mountain peaks – in most cases by the Italians, but in some cases also by Austro-Hungarian sappers. On 17 April 1916 the undermined peak of the Col di Lana was blown up by the Italians, killing about 200 Kaiserjägers.

Trench on Mount Vioz position, at an altitude of about 11,800 feet (3,600m). Apart from the nearest man – who has goggles, gloves, and apparently a snow cape slung ready on his back from tapes to his belt – these soldiers wear only standard infantry uniform with greatcoats, apparently lacking any special cold weather clothing. (Kriegsarchiv)

On 15 May the k.u.k. 11., and 3. Armeen launched their southwards offensive in the Tyrol. Despite success in taking mountain peaks and high altitude positions, the offensive failed to make progress in the valleys and came to a standstill on 16 June. Meanwhile, the Russian Gen Brusilov had launched an offensive in the East, and late in June Austro-Hungarian reinforcements had to be rushed to that front.

This gave the Italians a chance to counter-attack, and the Austro-Hungarian forces had to give up ground taken at high cost in order to shorten their front line. In August, during the Sixth Battle of the Isonzo, the Italians finally captured the town of Gorizia.

The (First) **Brusilov Offensive** by the Russian South-West Front – 7th, 8th, 9th and 11th Armies – had opened on 4 June 1916 to relieve Austro-Hungarian pressure on the Italian front. Britain and France were not yet ready to launch their own summer offensives, which would follow in July. The Russian plan was well co-ordinated among the Entente staffs, and well prepared and executed by

this most able of Russia's generals. Heralded by heavy and unusually sophisticated artillery bombardments, the Russian attack fell first on the k.u.k. 4. Armee, which was driven back behind the Styr river and lost the bridgehead at Luck on 7 June. On the southern flank the k.u.k. 7. Armee was hard pressed by the Russian 7th and 9th Armies and had to give way, exposing the eastern Bukovina and the entrance to the Carpathian passes. The town of Czernowitz was lost on 18 June. Brusilov's first offensive ran out of momentum with the arrival of reinforcements from the Balkans and southern Tyrol, having inflicted heavy losses on the badly shaken Austro-Hungarian armies.

To the north the offensive by Russia's West Front – in fact planned as the main effort, to which Brusilov's operations were supposedly secondary – opened on 2 July, but made little progress despite massive casualties. The next day Gen Brusilov launched his second offensive west of Luck, which was met and eventually halted by the k.u.k. 4. Armee. Costly fighting continued through August, as casualties mounted and Brusilov's lines of supply became overstretched. A counter-attack by the k.u.k. 7. Armee did not break through, but stabilised the area astride the borders of Russia, Galicia and Romania. In all the Austro-Hungarian forces had lost at least 150,000 men during this campaign.

On 27 August 1916, **Romania** declared war on the Austro-Hungarian Empire, and started operations to invade Siebenbürgen (Transylvania) from the Carpathian mountains with a force of about 400,000 men. The Austro-Hungarian defenders from k.u.k. 1. Armee numbered only about 35,000 in two divisions and six brigades, and had to make a fighting retreat to a second line. Nearly the same happened in the Dobrudja area, where about 140,000 Romanians faced 70,000 Germans and Bulgarians.

The combined k.u.k. 1. Armee and newly assembled German 9th Army met the Romanians, inflicted several defeats, and forced them back behind their borders by mid-October. In an attempt to relieve the pressure on the Romanians, Gen Brusilov launched a third offensive, but without success; it was halted in December 1916. Romania was invaded at the end of November, and the capital Bucharest fell to German troops on 6 December.

The end of an era

On 22 November 1916 the Emperor Franz Joseph I died in Vienna at the age of 86 years. His death not only marked the end of an era influenced by his long reign of 68 years; it removed Austro-Hungary's primary symbol of continuity, fellowship and unity. His successor on the throne, Karl I, faced a very difficult task.

A posed photograph from the trenches around the much-contested town of Gorizia on the lower Isonzo river front, autumn 1915. In this stony region the digging of trenches was nearly impossible; piled stone parapets gave some protection against infantry fire, but the extra fragmentation often proved deadly when they were hit by artillery.

The standard pattern pike-grey woollen field tunic is clearly shown here; note the deeply scalloped flaps of the patch breast pockets and internal hip pockets, and the large facing colour patches on the standing collar. Note both cloth-covered and uncovered cap peaks. (Kriegsarchiv)

OPPOSITE A member of the Austrian k.k. Gendarmerie serving in a police function at a bazaar in occupied Albania, 1916. Note on his left sleeve the brassard in the Austrian national colours – yellow/black/yellow – without an inscription. (Kriegsarchiv)

Isonzo front, 1915: Stabs-Feldwebel Stefan Paulic-Piljic of the 1st Battalion, Bosnian-Herzegovinian Infantry Regiment No.3. He proudly displays his Medal for Bravery; and note the red marksmanship lanyard peeping out from beneath his jacket. He is dressed in pike-grey, including the field version of the fez, and his neck band is typically folded out to cover part of the collar patches. These were in 'aliacin-red' facing colour for all four Bosnian-Herzegovinian regiments. His brass belt buckle plate shows the double-headed eagle motif; that for officers bore the imperial/royal cypher. The belt supports a small binocular case and the holster for a semi-automatic pistol, probably the Roth-Steyr 8mm M07. See Plate B3; and for details of the rank insignia see chart opposite, item 15. (Kriegsarchiv)

UNIFORMS & EQUIPMENT

Like most of the other European nations at the end of the 19th century, Austria-Hungary had a colourfully uniformed army. The last major changes, after 1866, had replaced the traditional costume – the white tunic of the infantry – with dark blue, which dominated the parade and campaign uniforms up to the early years of the 20th century.

In 1908 the next major change began to be seen, and for the first time this would affect the armed forces as a whole. Influenced by early 20th century wars elsewhere and convinced that the next conflict would be in the Balkans, the authorities introduced a new field uniform completely in a less conspicuous colour termed *hechtgrau* – 'pike-grey'. This shade was not itself newly invented, since it had been in use by the Jäger and technical troops for decades.

The soft, high-crowned field cap had a peak of black composition material, later often covered with grey cloth or painted grey; and a deep 'curtain' flap fastened by two regimental buttons in front, which could be let down to protect the face and neck. On the front of the crown all ranks wore a national cockade ('rosette') in plain metal, pierced with the imperial/royal monogram 'FJI' or (for Hungarian units) '1FJ'. The cavalry wore a peakless version of the field cap – virtually a sidecap.

The new jacket was produced in two versions: a woollen standard version with a standing collar, and a linen 'summer' version with a stand-and-fall collar. Interestingly, the summer version was less common among the troops than the standard woollen model. Wartime photographs frequently show the woollen version worn in summer, and the linen type mainly limited to use in the warmer southern areas, e.g. the Adriatic coast (lower Isonzo), Dalmatia, Montenegro and Albania. Both types had concealed buttons, and pairs of breast and hip pockets with scalloped flaps, again with the buttons concealed; however, photographs show that the pocket flaps – especially on the breast – sometimes had visible buttons (irregularly hand made?). The jacket had broad, square-ended shoulder straps, and a very typical Austro-Hungarian feature was a shoulder roll fixed at the outer end of the right shoulder strap in order to retain the slung or shouldered rifle. The matching trousers came in several patterns. Hungarian units had special lace trim – see Plate B2. Dismounted troops wore straight, loose trousers gathered at the ankle by small gaiters (Hosenspagen) fastened with buttons. Mountain troops and Landwehr wore knee breeches with long stockings, sometimes with long buttoned canvas gaiters. Foot artillery wore pantaloons, full in the thigh but tight below the knee; similar pantaloons were worn by Bosnian-Herzegovinian units. Mounted units wore breeches.

The new field uniform was accompanied by new leather equipment, which changed from black to natural brown, including the boots (though these were usually blackened with protective polish). Two weights of ankle boots were issued, the heavier type for mountain units; Pioneers wore 'jackboots' similar to the German 'marching boot'. The basis of the field equipment was a waist belt with four or two cartridge pouches and the frogged bayonet; and a natural hide knapsack in two parts, the upper holding the greatcoat, spare clothing and rations, the small lower compartment an ammunition reserve and a tinned soup

General officers (*Generale*, 1-5): Scarlet collar patch; gold embroidery **(1)** & zig-zag lace **(2-5)**; embroidered silver laurel wreath **(2)** and stars.

Field officers (*Stabs-Offiziere*, 6-9): Collar patch in regimental or branch facing colour; gold or silver embroidery & zig-zag lace corresponding to regimental or branch button colour; embroidered gold or silver stars opposite to lace colour; **(6)** small black patch on larger scarlet patch, gold lace, embroidered silver stars.

Captains & subalterns (*Ober-Offiziere*, 10-12): Collar patch in regimental or branch facing colour; embroidered gold or silver stars in regimental or branch button colour.

NCOs (*Unter-Offiziere*, 13-19): Collar patch in regimental or branch facing colour; **(13)** gold 1.3cm lace, silver metal star; **(14)** yellow silk 1.3cm lace, gold 0.6cm lace, silver metal star; **(15)** yellow silk 1.3cm lace with 0.2cm black central stripe, gold 0.6cm lace, white celluloid stars; **(16)** gold 1.3cm lace overlapping 1.3cm yellow lace; later, gold lace removed, remaining yellow lace as for **(18)**; white celluloid stars; small regimental or branch button from March 1915; **(17)** until March 1915, yellow cuff lace with black central stripe ; **(18)** yellow lace, **(18 & 19)** white celluloid stars.

Men (*Gemeine*, 20-22): Collar patch in regimental or branch facing colour, white celluloid stars.

(1) *Feldmarschall* (Field Marshal)
(2) *Generaloberst* (Colonel-General)
(3) *General der Infanterie* (General), Infantry
(4) *Feldmarschalleutnant* (Lieutenant-General)
(5) *Generalmajor* (Major-General)
(6) *Oberst* (Colonel), General Staff
(7) *Oberst* (Colonel)
(8) *Oberstleutnant* (Lieutenant Colonel)
(9) *Major* (Major)
(10) *Hauptmann* (Captain)
(11) *Oberleutnant* (Lieutenant)
(12) *Leutnant* (2nd Lieutenant)
(13) *Fähnrich* (Ensign, Warrant Officer I)
(14) *Offiziersstellvertreter* (WO II)
(15) *Stabs-Feldwebel* (Staff Sergeant-Major)
(16) *Einjährig Freiwilliger Kadettaspirant-Feldwebel* (One Year Volunteer Cadet Sergeant-Major)
(17) *Einjährig Freiwilliger* (One Year Volunteer)
(18) *Feldwebel* (Sergeant-Major)
(19) *Zugsführer* (Sergeant)
(20) *Korporal* (Corporal)
(21) *Gefreiter* (Lance-Corporal)
(22) *Infanterist* (Private)

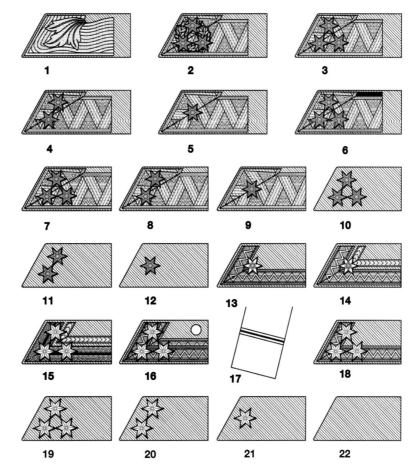

Notes:

(3) Cavalry = *General der Kavallerie*, Artillery = *Feldzeugmeister*

(10) Cavalry = *Rittmeister*

(13-22) NCOs' and mens' rank stars of regiments which had white facings were slightly smaller and had a backing of dark blue cloth.

(15) Jäger = *Stabs-Oberjäger*, Cavalry = *Stabs-Wachtmeister*, Artillery = *Stabs-Feuerwerker*

(16) E F Kadettaspirant-*Oberjäger*, -*Wachtmeister*, -*Feuerwerker* in Jäger, Cavalry, Artillery respectively

(18) *Oberjäger*, *Wachtmeister*, *Feuerwerker* in Jäger, Cavalry, Artillery respectively

(20) Jäger = *Unterjäger*

(21) Jäger = *Patrouillenführer*, Artillery = *Vormeister*

(22) Jäger = *Jäger*, Dragoons = *Dragoner*, Hussars = *Husar*, Ulans = *Ulan*, Artillery = *Kanonier*, Train & Medical Service = *Trainsoldat* & *Sanitätssoldat* respectively.

Drawings by Darko Pavlovic

ration. A tent section, pegs and poles were strapped to the knapsack. A slung haversack ('bread bag') contained a water bottle, eating utensils, the bread ration and some personal items. The soldier's total load in marching order was about 60lbs (27kg) – normal for most armies of the day. Half the men in each section also carried the Linneman entrenching spade, two men picks, and one a wire-cutter.

* * *

While the infantry and the technical troops more or less accepted this new uniform without much opposition, the cavalry arm managed to avoid its drab uniformity until the end of 1915. Theoretically, in August 1914 the whole army in the field should have been equipped with the new uniform; but thousands of photographs confirm that in reality the troops on campaign showed many individual differences, from the very first days and for a considerable time thereafter. The reason was quite simple. The professional officers, who purchased their own uniforms and equipment, always tried to be dressed and equipped *à la mode,* and were usually allowed some latitude over individual items such as privately tailored jackets showing differently cut collars, the choice of pistols or revolvers, binoculars, boots, and so forth. The professional NCOs sometimes tried to copy their officers. The rank and file were completely dressed by the depots; but despite regulation issues even they managed to add some personal touches – e.g. by

Trench scene on the Galician front, late spring 1916. The soldiers are dressed in the early version of the field-grey uniform with the jacket cut similar to the pike-grey model. Note that puttees were becoming increasingly popular. They look cheerful enough in this quiet, sunny sector. Typically the Austro-Hungarian infantryman was a rural peasant, accustomed to long days of labour in the open air for little return. His pay was abysmal, his conditions of service hard and his discipline severe; but the Army had a patriarchal ethos, and searching post-war enquiries by a Socialist commission failed to confirm any allegations of brutality by officers. (Kriegsarchiv)

covering the upper part of the collar and its insignia with the folded-over internal neck band (also in pike-grey) which was introduced with the M1908 field uniform.

This latter fashion, uniquely, sometimes proved life-saving when it hid part of the colourful collar insignia from enemy snipers; most individual touches had the opposite effect. The officers' taste for the idle but fashionable use of old distinctions included the black and yellow field sashes of staff and infantry officers, the diagonal *Kartuscheriemen* pouch belt of cavalry and artillery officers, shiny leather gaiters, polished boots and dazzling sabres – all of which quickly proved lethally attractive to enemy marksmen, who killed them in hundreds. In September 1914 the Archduke Friedrich issued a circular letter recommending officers to keep a low profile and to avoid wearing sashes and even leather gaiters. Following these instructions, sabres were either left behind or, in many cases, at least had their shiny scabbards darkened.

The same document also brought to an end the long history of drummers within the infantry; modern warfare had proved them useless on the battlefield. The drums were to be sent back to the depots and the drummers became ordinary soldiers within their units. During the same period another long preserved Austro-Hungarian peculiarity began to fade away. Traditionally, the emperor's troops had worn a special field sign – an oakleaf in summer and a fir twig in winter – fastened behind their hat cockades. With the new M1908 field uniform these were ordered to be placed on the left side of the cap, helmet or fez (the latter of the Muslim Bosnian and Herzegovinian troops). In summer 1914 the troops proudly wore the field sign during the first weeks of the conflict, but photographs show that as early as the late autumn of 1914 it had virtually disappeared, and thereafter was seen only during ceremonies, inspections and parades.

Within a short time, however, another typically Austro-Hungarian habit was adopted by both officers and other ranks: the fixing of metal badges along the left side of the field cap. These badges – of brass or white metal and sometimes even enamelled in colours – were usually sold by canteens and other army stores. Many of them featured regimental symbols or references to campaigns; to individuals such as the emperor, archdukes, or commanding generals; to patriotic scenes, propaganda images, or even religious motifs. Others were sold to raise funds for charity groups. By 1918 hundreds of different types had been produced and had found their way onto the soldiers' headdress.

*   *   *

Like most of the other armies engaged in the Great War, Austria-Hungary did not have sufficient stocks in her depots to support long campaigns. In August 1914 everyone thought that they would be home by Christmas, at the latest. Consequently, from late autumn 1914 the priority for clothing the Austro-Hungarian forces ceased to be the correct adherence to written regulations and became much more a matter of using what was to hand. While everyone tried to get warm clothing for the forthcoming winter, the administration tried to stan-dardise different uniform parts in order to achieve more efficiency when ordering replacements. Among the first innovations were the 'unified' trousers of 1915; the *Kniehose* ('knee length trousers' – in fact, longer) of the Landwehr were adopted as a common garment. From that time the

A Schwarzlose M07/12 machine gun in a trench position near Wladimir-Wolinski, 1916; the folding 7mm steel shield has been removed to save weight. This water-cooled 8mm weapon was the standard machine gun used throughout the war on all fronts; its tripod mount could be adjusted to allow fire either at or about two feet above ground level, like that of the German MG08. In 1914 the regimental machine gun company had four sections each with two guns; of the five officers and 157 men, 46 were drivers for the company's 16 horses, 24 mules and seven wagons. The officers, 80 men and the pack animals formed the combat echelon, the rest the company ammunition train.

Machine gun crews were usually armed with semi-automatic pistols, the most common being the 8mm Roth-Steyr M07 and the 9mm M12 *Repetierpistole* (the so-called 'Steyr 12'). Note the holster with external pouch for a spare clip; both pistols had fixed magazines, and cartridges had to be loaded from a stripper clip like that of the 'broomhandle' Mauser. (Kriegsarchiv)

distinctive Hungarian trousers gradually fell victim to the issue of the new type, which could be worn with both *Wadenstutzen* (woollen stockings) or the puttees which were becoming increasingly popular.

Apart from these major changes, small stylistic items like the feathers decorating the caps of the mountain formations still remained in use, and were even expanded by a newly raised formation: the Grenzjägertruppe in the Balkans, who proudly displayed eagle feathers in their caps.

The pike-grey uniform colour proved unsuitable on the Galician plains, and this may have influenced the authorities to consider alternatives. In autumn 1915 they settled on the choice of introducing the German *feldgrau* (field-grey) for the Austro-Hungarian forces. This was often referred to alternatively as *feldgrün* (field-green), perhaps to emphasise national differences.

With the introduction of field-grey/field-green the cut of the jacket (Bluse) was initially unchanged; but a new type soon began to replace both the 1908 models and the early field-grey. This retained concealed buttons but had a more comfortable stand-and-fall collar. Already in use for some time, it was formally adopted as the Einheitsbluse M16 that autumn. From the first, shortages of coloured cloth made it necessary to reduce the size of the collar patches in regimental facing colours (see under 'The Infantry' below, and Table 1); by 1916/17 these had shrunk to simple vertical stripes behind any rank devices, which were retained until the end of the war.

While newly raised units were usually issued complete field-grey uniforms before marching out, the troops already at the front at first received field-grey items as replacement garments only. Consequently, all kinds of combinations of pike-grey and field-grey might be seen, especially between late 1915 and 1916.

At the beginning of operations in summer 1914 pike-grey uniforms were only available for first line troops of the Common Army, the Landwehr and Honvéd. The Landsturm formations were usually fitted out with pre-1908 uniforms; and in August 1914 some units even went on campaign wearing civilian clothes with a brassard of yellow/black/yellow (or for Hungarians, green/white/red) on their left arm to indicate their status as regular soldiers. These shortages, from the very beginning of the war, were a first warning of many more problems to be faced during the years to come.

Weapons

The regulation issue for the infantry was the 8mm M95 Mannlicher rifle, with shorter carbine versions for mounted, mountain and technical troops. However, there were still many of the older 8mm M90 and M88/90 Mannlichers available, and these were frequently issued to Landsturm and replacement troops. Units guarding depots in the rear areas were sometimes issued Werndl 11mm M67/77 and M73/77 rifles. Since Austria-Hungary also produced Mauser rifles under licence for export, stocks were made available for the armed forces in 1914. The 7mm so-called 'Mexican' Mauser (produced for the Mexican government) came into use in great numbers; as the war continued other types were also to be seen, including rifles originally produced for Romania and Greece, as well as captured Russian weapons.

Handguns were either issued or purchased privately by officers before the war. The most common of many models in use included the eight-shot 8mm Rast & Gasser M98 Armeerevolver for the infantry, the 8mm Roth-Krnka M07 Repetierpistole for the cavalry, and the old 11mm Gasser M70 and 70/74 Armeerevolver for the artillery and train units. The 9mm Steyr M12 Repetierpistole and 9mm Gasser-Kropatschek revolver also came into common use, while staff officers often preferred lighter weapons such as the 7.65mm Steyr-Kipplaufpistole or 7.65mm Frommer-Stop pistol. The most accepted pistol among the aviation troops was the classic 7.63mm Mauser C96 'broomhandle' with its wooden holster/shoulder stock. Generally, after the war started practically any handgun might be found among the troops, either home produced or captured.

Heavy weapons included the 8mm Schwarzlose M07/12 machine gun which remained the standard issue but, again, during the war a number of captured weapons also came into use on the different fronts, such as the Italian Fiat-Revelli and the Russian Maxim. Support weapons such as trench mortars or infantry guns were not employed in 1914 but developed during the first two years of war, especially after experience of facing such weapons in the hands of the Russian forces. From the end of 1915 trench mortars came into frequent use on practically all fronts, their calibres varying from 9cm to 26cm (the heavier calibres not being used by the infantry). Common early types were the 9cm M15 and M16 Minenwerfer, firing bombs weighing respectively 5.5kg (12¾lbs) and 11kg (23¼lbs); these had the disadvantage of a highly visible muzzle flash. The two-mortar detachment usually numbered about 30 men with a subaltern and two NCOs. A pair of light, short range 3.7cm M15 and later M16 'infantry guns' was also introduced at regimental level from 1916, operated by a section of similar size drawn from specially trained infantrymen; they fired 0.55kg (1¼lb) shells out to ranges of just over a mile (1,800m).

Zugsführer (sergeant) and soldier of the k.k. Tiroler Landesschützen, with climbing equipment including ropes, ice pick and snow shoes. The blackcock feather on the cap and the Edelweiss badge on the green collar patches were distinctive of these troops. See Plate E2. (Kriegsarchiv)

Table 1: Austro-Hungarian Common Army Infantry Regiments, 1914

(G = 'German' regiment, H = 'Hungarian'; W = buttons white metal, Y = yellow metal)

No. Title	Recruiting area	Facing colour	Buttons
1 Kaiser	Troppau (G)	dark red	Y
2 Alexander I., Kaiser von Rußland	Brassó (H)	imperial yellow	Y
3 Erzherzog Carl	Kremsier (G)	sky-blue	W
4 Hoch- und Deutschmeister	Wien (G)	sky-blue	Y
5 Freiherr von Klobucar	Szatmár-Németi (H)	rose-red	Y
6 Carl I, König von Rumänien	Ujvidék (H)	rose-red	W
7 Graf von Khevenhüller	Klagenfurt (G)	dark brown	W
8 Erzherzog Carl Stephan	Brünn (G)	grass-green	Y
9 Graf Clerfayt	Stryj (G)	apple-green	Y
10 Gustav V, König von Schweden,	Przemysl (G)	parrot-green	W
11 Johann Prinz zu Sachsen	Pisek (G)	ash-grey	Y
12 Parmann	Komárom (H)	dark brown	Y
13 Jung-Starhemberg	Krakau (G)	rose-red	Y
14 Ernst Ludwig, Großherzog von Hessen u.bei Rhein	Linz (G)	black	Y
15 Freiherr von Georgi	Tarnopol (G)	madder-red	Y
16 Freiherr von Giesl (Warasdiner IR)	Belovar (H)	sulphur-yellow	Y
17 Ritter von Milde	Laibach (G)	red-brown	W
18 Erzherzog Leopold Salvator	Königgrätz (G)	dark red	W
19 Erzherzog Franz von Preußen	Györ (H)	sky-blue	W
20 Heinrich Prinz von Preußen	Neusandez (G)	lobster-red	W
21 Graf von Abensperg u. Traun	Caslau (G)	sea-green	Y
22 Graf von Lacy	Sinj (G)	imperial yellow	W
23 Markgraf von Baden	Zambor (H)	cherry-red	W
24 Ritter von Kummer	Kolomea	ash-grey	W
25 Edler von Pokorny	Losoncz (H)	sea-green	W
26 Schreiber	Esztergom (H)	black	Y
27 Albert I, König der Belgien	Graz (G)	imperial yellow	Y
28 Viktor Emanuel III, König von Italien	Prague (G)	grass-green	W
29 Freiherr von Loudon	Nagybecskerek (H)	light blue	W
30 Schoedler	Lemberg (G)	pike-grey	Y
31 Pucherna	Nagyszeben (H)	imperial yellow	W
32 Kaiserin u. Königin Maria Theresia	Budapest (H)	sky-blue	W
33 Kaiser Leopold I	Arad (H)	ash-grey	Y
34 Wilhelm I, Deutscher Kaiser u König von Preußen	Kassa (H)	madder-red	W
35 Freiherr von Sterneck	Pilsen (G)	lobster-red	Y
36 Reichsgraf Browne	Jungbunzlau (G)	pale red	W
37 Erzherzog Josef	Nagy-Várad (H)	scarlet	Y
38 Alfons XIII, König von Spanien	Kecskemét (H)	black	W
39 Freiherr von Conrad	Debreczen (H)	scarlet	W
40 Ritter von Pino	Rzeszów (G)	light blue	Y
51 von Boroevic	Kolzsvár (H)	ash-grey	Y
52 Erzherzog Friedrich	Pécs (H)	dark red	Y
53 Dankl	Agram (H)	dark red	W
54 Alt-Starhemberg	Olmütz (G)	apple-green	W
55 Nikolaus I, König von Montenegro	Brzezany (G)	red-brown	Y
56 Graf Daun	Wadowice (G)	steel-green	Y
57 Prinz zu Sachsen-Coburg-Saalfeld	Tarnów (G)	pale red	Y
58 Erzherzog Ludwig Salvator	Stanislau (G)	black	W
59 Erzherzog Rainer	Salzburg (G)	orange-yellow	W
60 Ritter von Ziegler	Eger/Ungarn (H)	steel-green	W
61 Ritter von Frank	Temesvár (H)	grass-green	Y
62 Ludwig III, König von Bayern	Maros-Vásárhely (H)	grass-green	W
63 Freiherr von Pitreich	Besztercze (H)	orange-yellow	W
64 Ritter von Auffenberg	Szászváros	orange-yellow	Y
65 Erzherzog Ludwig Viktor	Munkács (H)	pale red	Y
66 Erzherzog Peter Ferdinand	Ungvár (H)	pale red	W
67 Freiherr Kray	Eperjes (H)	lobster-red	W
68 Freiherr von Reicher	Szolnok (H)	red-brown	Y
69 Freiherr von Leithner	Székesfehérvár (H)	pike-grey	W
70 Edler von Appel (Peterwardein IR)	Peterwardein (H)	sea-green	Y
71 Galgótzy	Trencsén (H)	lobster-red	Y
72 Freiherr von David	Pozsony (H)	light blue	Y
73 Albrecht Herzog von Württemberg	Eger/Böhmen (G)	cherry-red	W
74 Freiherr von Schönaich	Jicin (G)	madder-red	W
75 *Title vacant*	Neuhaus (G)	light blue	W
76 Freiherr von Salis-Soglio	Sopron (H)	light blue	Y
77 Philipp Herzog von Württemberg	Sambor (G)	cherry-red	W
78 Gerba	Esseg (H)	red-brown	W
79 Graf Jellacic (Otocaner IR)	Otocac (H)	apple-green	W
80 Wilhelm Ernst Großherzog von Sachsen-Weimar-Eisenach, Herzog zu Sachsen	Zloczów (G)	scarlet	W
81 (Johann) Freiherr von Waldstätten	Iglau (G)	carmine	W
82 Freiherr von Schwitzer	Székélyudvarhely (H)	carmine	W
83 Freiherr von Schikofsky	Szombathely (H)	dark brown	W
84 Freiherr von Bolfras	Wien (G)	carmine	Y
85 von Gaudernak	Mármarossziget (H)	apple-green	Y
86 Freiherr von Steininger	Szabadka (H)	amaranth-red	Y
87 Freiherr von Succovaty	Cilli (G)	sea-green	W
88 *Title vacant*	Beraun (G)	bordeaux-red	W
89 Freiherr von Albori	Gródek-Jagiellonskii (G)	bordeaux-red	Y
90 Edler von Horsetzky	Jaroslau (G)	amaranth-red	Y
91 *Title vacant*	Budweis (G)	parrot-green	Y
92 Edler von Hortstein	Komotau (G)	white	W

No. & Honorary Colonel	Garrison	Facing colour	Button
93 Title vacant	Mährisch-Schönberg (G)	dark brown	Y
94 Freiherr von Koller	Turnau (G)	white	Y
95 von Kövess	Czortków (G)	amaranth-red	W
96 Ferdinand Kronprinz von Rumänien	Carlstadt (H)	carmine	Y
97 (Georg) Freiherr von Waldstätten	Trieste (G)	rose-red	W
98 von Rummer	Hohenmauth (G)	light fawn	W
99 Title vacant	Znaim (G)	sulphur-yellow	Y
100 von Steinsberg	Teschen (G)	light fawn	Y
101 Freiherr von Crahtschmidt	Békéscsaba (H)	sulphur-yellow	W
102 Potiorek	Beneschau (G)	sea-grass-green	Y
41 Erzherzog Eugen	Czernowitz (G)	sulphur-yellow	W
42 Ernst August Herzog von Cumberland, Herzog zu Braunschweig u.Lüneburg	Theresienstadt (G)	orange-yellow	W
43 Rupprecht Kronprinz von Bayern	Karánsebes (H)	cherry-red	Y
44 Erzherzog Albrecht	Kaposvár (H)	madder-red	Y
45 Erzherzog Josef Ferdinand	Sanok (G)	scarlet	Y
46 Title vacant	Szeget (H)	parrot-green	Y
47 Graf von Beck-Rzikowsky	Marburg (G)	steel-green	W
48 Rohr	Nagykanizsa (H)	steel-green	Y
49 Freiherr von Hess	St Pölten (G)	pike-grey	W
50 Friedrich Großherzog von Baden	Gyulafehérvár (H)	parrot-green	W

Hand grenades of several models were developed, and at first were as improvised and unreliable as those of other combatant armies. Two main types officially issued from March 1915, in parallel with increasingly widespread supplies of the German stick grenade, were an 'egg' type, and the Rohr grenade. The latter was a short cast iron cylinder weighing 0.8kg (1lb 13oz), enclosed in a cardboard tube which served as a throwing handle, and ignited by a 4- or 8-second friction pull fuze.

Additional equipment such as flame-throwers and items for gas warfare were developed during the war by special formations of the k.u.k. Sappeurtruppe and came into use from 1916.

Lastly, the special items issued for **mountain warfare** should be mentioned. The status of mountain equipment in 1914 was at its best among the specialist units raised from Alpine regions such as the Tyrol and Carinthia. In 1914 seven regiments – all from the k.k. Landwehr – were specially trained and equipped for this type of warfare: the Tyrolean Landeschützenregimenter I (Trient), II (Bozen) and III (Innichen); the k.k. Landwehrinfanterieregimenter No.4 (Klagenfurt) and No. 27 (Laibach), to be re-named Gebirgsschützenregimenter Nos.1 & 2 in 1917; and the k.k. Landwehrinfanterieregimenter Nos.23 (Zara) and 37 (Gravosa), both from Dalmatia.

With the exception of the Dalmatians these units all wore the distinctive *Birkhahn* (blackcock) feather in their caps and the *Edelweiss* symbol on their collar patches. Their uniforms were specially cut in a practical 'sportsman' style for mountain climbing; their equipment included heavy boots, snow goggles, snow shoes, skis, ice picks and climbing ropes, along with an Alpine type of overcoat specially designed to protect both man and equipment in severe weather conditions. Additionally, these troops also made wide use of snow camouflage smocks of various different designs during the winters along the Italian front (although these were in fact first seen in winter 1914/15 in Galicia and the Carpathians, used by infantry and cavalry units).

THE INFANTRY

As in all other nations of the period, the infantry formed the main mass of troops for operations. The last peacetime order of battle registered 110 regiments of infantry for the Common Army, made up of 102 Line regiments each with 4 field battalions; 4 regiments of Tiroler Kaiser-jäger (Regts Nos.1, 3 & 4 with 3 bns, No.2 with 4 bns); and 4 Bosnian-Herzegovinian regiments (Nos.1-3 with 4 bns, No.4 with 3 battalions).

Additional units included 26 Feldjäger (rifle) battalions; one Bosnian-Herzegovinian Feldjäger battalion; 6 Grenzjäger companies (established in late spring 1914); 37 k.k. Landwehr infantry regiments (usually with 3 field bns, except No.4 with 5 bns, No.23 with 2 bns, and No.27 with 4 bns); 3 Tyrolean k.k. Landesschützen regiments (No.I with 6 bns, Nos.II & III with 5 bns each); and 32 k.u. Honvéd infantry regiments (usually with 3 field bns, only No.19 having 4 battalions).

The Landsturm formed 40 regiments (a total of 136 battalions) in the Austrian half of the Empire, and in the Hungarian regions 32 regiments (totalling 97 battalions).

The 1914 war establishment of the infantry regiment was up to 4,600 all ranks, organised in a small regimental staff; a Pioneer platoon; four battalions, each of four rifle companies (each 5 officers, 250 men), each of four platoons; and four machine gun sections (each 1 officer, 36 men, 2 guns). The establishment of the Jäger battalion was a headquarters, a Pioneer platoon, four companies each of four platoons, and one machine-gun section.

Insignia

The historical system of identifying infantry regiments by facing colours – now reduced to collar patches – and buttons of either white or yellow metal was still in use in summer 1914. The administration separated the infantry regiments into two blocks: the 'German' regiments, from the Austrian part of the Dual Monarchy but including Galicians, Bohemians, Italians, etc.; and the 'Hungarian' regiments, also including Croatians, and Romanians from Transylvania. The Hungarian regiments could easily be identified by their distinctive trousers, decorated on the thigh with the *vitez-kötes* or Hungarian knot. Therefore, four regiments could share the same facing colour: two 'German' and two 'Hungarian', one of each pair having yellow metal and the other white metal buttons. The collar insignia also incorporated badges of rank as appropriate (see chart on page 17).

The system looks simple, but in fact the bureaucracy created a range of facing colours such as 'parrot-green', 'bordeaux-red' (wine red), or 'rose-red' (practically a shade of pink) which made confident identification a matter for specialists only. The regimental titles, facings and button colours of the Common Army regiments are listed in Table 1 on pages 22-23.

The Tyrolean Kaiserjäger regiments all displayed the 'grass-green' facing of the Jäger units. The 26 independent Feldjäger battalions and the Bosnian-Herzegovinian Jäger battalion in 1914 used the same facing colour. The four Bosnian-Herzegovinian infantry regiments shared the facing colour 'aliacin-red', and were distinguishable by the regimental number on their buttons. The Austrian Landwehr all had grass-green facing colour, whereas the Hungarian Honvéd all displayed slate-grey.

The system worked quite well as long as the Army as a whole was a 'colourful institution'. With the introduction of drab field uniforms only the facing colour collar patches remained clearly visible; buttons appeared only on the shoulder straps and were later darkened to reduce visibility. The identification of regiments at a glance thus became impossible, and even more problematic from the mid-war years when the collar patches were reduced to simple stripes.

Interesting variations were displayed by the four Bosnian-Herzegovinian infantry regiments and the Jäger battalion from this region. Their usual headdress was the Muslim fez, but for Christian officers the wearing of the fez was optional. In practice, most of the officers adopted the fez, both to show solidarity with their men

A classic study of an Austro-Hungarian infantryman of a 'German' regiment in 1914, wearing the 1908 pike-grey field uniform; note that his neck band is turned down outside the collar, partly hiding the collar patch in regimental facing colour. The loosely cut trousers are gathered at the ankle with two-button gaiters. He is armed with the 8mm M95 Mannlicher rifle, a 'straight pull' bolt action weapon with a five-round fixed magazine; it measures 50in long overall and weighs just over 8.3lbs. The field equipment is in natural brown leather; the four cartridge pouches – hidden here – contained 40 rounds, and another 80 were carried in the lower section of the two-part knapsack. Note the tent section rolled and strapped around his knapsack, and the 'bread bag' slung on his left hip – this contained the water bottle. (Author's collection)

(continued on page 34)

SUMMER 1914

1: Hauptmann, k.u.k. IR No.4 'Hoch- und Deutschmeister', summer 1914
2: Hauptmann im Generalstabskorps, summer 1914
3: Oberleutnant der Artillerie

A

1: Korporal, k.u.k. IR No.27 'Albert I, König der Belgier', summer 1914
2: Zugsführer, k.u.k. IR No.53 'General Dankl'
3: Feldwebel, k.u.k bosnisch-herzegowinisches IR No.4
4: Tambour, k.u.k. IR No.97 'Freiherr von Waldstätten'

B

1: Korporal, k.u.k. Dragonerregiment No.10 'Fürst von Liechtenstein'
2: Ulan, k.u.k. Ulanenregiment No.2 'Fürst zu Schwarzenberg'
3: Wachtmeister, k.u.k. Husarenregiment No.13 'Friedrich Wilhelm
   Kronprinz des Deutschen Reiches und Kronprinz von Preussen'
4: Zugsführer-Trompeter, k.u. Honvéd Husarenregiment No.4

C

AUTUMN/WINTER 1914/15
1: Austrian Landsturmmann, autumn/winter
   1914/15
2: General Staff officer improvised winter uniform;
   Capathian Mountains, winter 1914/15
3: Infantryman in marching order, winter 1914/15

NACH PRZEMYSL

D

1: Korporal, k.k. Landwehr-IR No.4 Klagenfurt, spring 1915
2: Tyrolean *Landesschütze* with ski equipment
3: Schütze, Kärntner Freiwillige Schützen, autumn 1916
4: Tyrolean Standschütze, autumn 1915/spring 1916

E

1: Sapper, Isonzo front, early 1916
2: Austrian Feldgendarm, Isonzo front, 1915/16
3: Officer, Royal Hungarian Gendarmerie (Mounted), winter 1915/16
4: Gefreiter, k.k. Landwehr-IR No.23; Gorizia, spring 1916

F

1: Zugskommandant, Polish Legion, late 1915
2: Ulan, Polish Legion, mid-1915
3: Soldier, Polish Legion infantry, late 1914
4: Legions-Zugskommandant,
   Ukrainian Legion, autumn 1916

G

1: Kanonier, 24cm Motor-Mörserbatterie No.9; Gallipoli, winter 1915/16
2: Major, 15cm Haubitzbatterie No.36; Smyrna, spring 1916
3: Zugsführer, Gebirgshaubitzdivision von Marno; Palestine, summer 1916
4: Korporal, Autokolonne Türkei No.2; Diarbekhir, summer/autumn 1916

H

Table 2: The Cavalry Regiments

DRAGOONS

No.	Title	Area	Facing colour	Buttons
1	Kaiser Franz	Leitmeritz	dark red	white
2	Graf Paar	Prag	black	white
3	Friedrich August König von Sachsen	Wien	dark red	yellow
4	Kaiser Ferdinand	Innsbruck	grass green	white
5	Nikolaus I, Kaiser von Rußland	Graz	imperial yellow	white
6	Friedrich Franz IV. Großherzog von Mecklenburg-Schwerin	Wien	black	yellow
7	Herzog von Lothringen	Prag	sulphur yellow	white
8	Graf Montecuccoli	Leitmeritz	scarlet	yellow
9	Erzherzog Albrecht	Lemberg	grass green	yellow
10	Fürst von Liechtenstein	Prag	sulphur yellow	yellow
11	Kaiser	Wien	scarlet	white
12	Nikolaus Nikolajewitsch Großfürst von Rußland	Krakau	imperial yellow	yellow
13	Eugen Prinz von Savoyen	Leitmeritz	madder red	white
14	Fürst zu Windisch-Graetz	Prag	madder red	yellow
15	Erzherzog Joseph	Wien	white	yellow

HUSSARS

No.	Title	Area	Attila	Olives	Shako
1	Kaiser	Temesvár	dark blue	yellow	dark blue
2	Friedrich Leopold Prinz von Preußen	Nagyszeben	light blue	yellow	white
3	Graf von Hadik	Temesvár	dark blue	yellow	white
4	Artur Herzog von Connaught und Strathearn	Temesvár	light blue	white	madder red
5	Graf Radetzky	Pozsony	dark blue	white	madder red
6	Wilhelm II. König von Württemberg	Kassa	light blue	yellow	ash grey
7	Wilhelm II. Deutscher Kaiser und König von Preußen	Budapest	light blue	white	light blue
8	von Tersztyánszky	Budapest	dark blue	yellow	madder red
9	Graf Nádasdy	Pozsony	dark blue	white	white
10	Friedrich Wilhelm III. n König von Preuße	Budapest	light blue	yellow	light blue
11	Ferdinand I. König der Bulgaren	Pozsony	dark blue	white	ash grey
12	vacant	Kassa	light blue	white	white
13	Jazygier und Kumanier Husaren- regiment Wilhelm Kronprinz des Deutschen Reiches und Kronprinz von Preußen	Budapest	dark blue	white	dark blue
14	von Kolossváry	Kassa	light blue	yellow	madder red
15	Erzherzog Franz Salvator	Kassa	dark blue	yellow	ash grey
16	Graf Üxküll - Gyllenbrand	Temesvár	light blue	white	ash grey

ULANS

No.	Title	Area	Czapka	Buttons
1	Ritter von Brudermann	Krakau	imperial yellow	yellow
2	Fürst zu Schwarzenberg	Krakau	dark green	yellow
3	Erzherzog Carl	Przemysl	madder red	yellow
4	Kaiser	Lemberg	white	yellow
5	Nikolaus II. Kaiser von Rußland	Agram	light blue	yellow
6	Kaiser Joseph II.	Przemysl	imperial yellow	white
7	Erzherzog Franz Ferdinand	Lemberg	dark green	white
8	Graf Auersperg	Lemberg	madder red	white
9	not existing			
10	not existing			
11	Alexander II. Kaiser von Rußland	Leitmeritz and Przemysl	cherry red	white
12	Graf Huyn	Agram	dark blue	yellow
13	von Böhm-Ermolli	Lemberg	dark blue	white

and as a welcome difference from the rest of the Army. This distinction largely disappeared with the later general adoption of the steel helmet.

THE CAVALRY

The cavalry was the most traditionalist and conservative arm on the Austro-Hungarian armed forces, some of the regiments tracing their lineage back as far as the Thirty Years' War of the 17th century. The greatest modernising reform of the cavalry units was instituted after 1867 when the heaviest arm, the Cuirassiers, were disbanded and these regiments were converted to Dragoons. Furthermore, the practical distinctions between heavy and light cavalry vanished, and the remaining three types of regiment – Dragoons, Hussars and Ulans (the Austrian spelling) – continued carrying the same arms consisting of carbines, revolvers (later semi-automatic pistols) and sabres only.

In 1914 they still wore their distinctive uniforms with helmets, shakos and czapkas, blue tunics, Attilas and Ulankas, all with red trousers (for Hussars, in Hungarian style). The Dragoon units were identified by different facing colours and buttons, while Hussars and Ulans were distinguishable by their shako and czapka colours. In the case of the Hussars half the regiments wore light blue uniforms (Attilas) and half dark blue; again, buttons in white or yellow metal made further distinctions. The Ulans all had madder-red collars and cuffs, and made further distinctions by the top colours of the czapka and the button metal.

During the early years of the 20th century machine gun and telegraph detachments had been formed and specially trained. To some extent, the machine gun detachments of the Dragoons and Ulans were the only cavalry troops to wear a pike-grey field uniform in 1914.

The peacetime organisation counted 15 regiments of Dragoons, 16 regiments of Hussars and 11 regiments of Ulans (Nrs.1-8 and 11-13). See Table 2, page 33, for regimental titles and facing colours. The normal strength of a cavalry regiment comprised six squadrons with 900 horses. In wartime the regiments were organised in Kavalleriedivisionen, each consisting of four regiments separated into two cavalry brigades.

In addition to the Common Army cavalry, the k.k. Landwehr had six regiments of Ulans, a division of mounted Tyrolean Landesschützen and another of mounted Dalmatian Landesschützen (each of two squadrons). The Hungarian Honvéd included ten Hussar regiments, and additional squadrons of Hungarian Landsturm Hussars.

It became evident during the early stages of the war that these formations were destined to suffer great losses. Hastily, at least some field items were created, sometimes 'on the spot'; the helmets of the Dragoons were either over-painted in grey or covered with grey linen, as were the shakos of

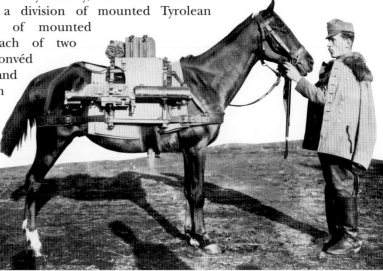

Pack-horse of a cavalry machine gun detachment; members of these and the telegraph detachments were the only cavalry troops to wear the pike-grey field uniform in 1914. The machine gun is the standard Schwarzlose M07/12; the tripod is attached on the far side of the pack saddle, and note ammunition boxes for the 250-round belts on top. Infantry MG sections used pack mules. (Kriegsarchiv)

the Hussars and the czapkas of the Ulans; sabre scabbords were also sometimes overpainted grey. Paradoxically, many Ulans still wore the high horsehair plume and brass chin chain with their field-covered czapkas. A further step was the 'overpainting' of the trumpeters' traditionally white horses; this led to some strange effects, like black-overpainted horses shining violet after the first contact with rain.

As the war continued it became difficult to supply remounts to keep up with the casualties among the horses, and each year a larger proportion of the cavalry were dismounted to serve as infantry in the trenches. Although they were issued field-grey uniforms from the second half of 1915, photographs show officers and men still wearing the winter overcoats of their old coloured uniforms. In reality the summer and autumn of 1914 saw the swansong of this old arm of service. It was on 21 August 1914 at Jaroslavice that the Dragoons and Ulans of the 4.Kavalleriedivision fought with distinction against Cossacks, Dragoons, Hussars and Ulans of the Russian 10th Cavalry Division, in what was later called the last true cavalry battle in history.

ARTILLERY, TECHNICAL & SPECIALIST TROOPS

The artillery arm had a remarkable tradition of devotion and ability, and had often distinguished itself in battle; for instance, in 1866 at Königgrätz, where a sacrificial stand by the major part of the artillery covered the retreat of the Austrian army. Nevertheless, before 1914 the importance of the artillery was underestimated in contrast to that of the cavalry, which was overvalued by the general staff. As a consequence, in summer 1914 the Austro-Hungarian divisions were mostly under-provided with artillery: a regular infantry division normally had only 46 pieces, in contrast to the German norm of 60, the Russians' 50 and the French Army's scale of 72 guns. Of even the 46 guns which were provided, at least 16 were old models that could no longer meet the demands of modern warfare. After the outbreak of war the artillery improved steadily, and within a relatively short period received modern and functionally suitable pieces.

The artillery was essentially divided into three branches: the field artillery (and horse artillery, with the cavalry divisions), mountain artillery, and fortress artillery. Among the many different pieces in use by field and mountain units the most notable were the 8cm and later 10.4cm field guns, 10cm and 15cm field howitzers, 7cm and 7.5cm mountain guns, and 10cm mountain howitzers. The mountain artillery formed a distinct branch and, as war proceeded, became famous for its valuable contribution on all fronts. The mountain guns could be disassembled

Loading a 30.5cm mortar of a mobile heavy artillery regiment on the Galician front. Note the variety of the footwear, including ankle boots with long stockings and puttees, 'jackboots', and (right) the officer's gaiters. The rear view of the greatcoat shows it large expansion pleat and buttoned rear half-belt for adjustment. (Kriegsarchiv)

easily for transport on pack horses. These guns and howitzers proved effective not only in mountain warfare but also in the deserts of southern Palestine, in the Balkans and on the Isonzo and later Piave fronts.

The fortress artillery, organised in battalions and companies, manned the pieces mounted in fortresses and fixed defences along the borders of the Empire, such as Przemysl in Galicia, and the impressive defensive line following the Italian border through the Dolomites and in Carinthia. As the war proceeded, with its new demands for the heavy bombardment of continuous trench systems, elements of the fortress artillery were made mobile to form 'heavy artillery regiments'. Types used by both the fortress and the heavy artillery included the 24cm M98/07 mortar (the German term – not to be confused with the British and American usage to mean a small trench mortar), which also saw action on the Gallipoli Peninsula and later in Palestine 1915–18; and perhaps the best known Austro-Hungarian piece of all, the 30.5cm M11/16 mortar. The heaviest pieces included 24cm and 35cm guns (the latter actually a naval gun), and the 38cm and 42cm howitzers.

In summer 1914 the main body of the artillery counted 42 Feldkanonenregimenter (field gun regiments), and 14 Feldhaubitz-regimenter (field howitzer regiments); 9 reitende Artillerie divisionen (horse artillery divisions, each with 2 or 3 batteries); 7 schwere Haubitzdivisionen (heavy howitzer divisions); 10 Gebirgsartillerie-regimenter (mountain artillery regiments); 6 Festungsartillerie-regimenter (fortress artillery regiments) and 8 Festungsartillerie-bataillone (fortress artillery battalions); 8 and Landwehrfeld-kanonen-divisionen, 8 Landwehrfeldhaubitz-divisionen, 8 Honvédfeldartillerieregimenter, and 1 Honvéd reitende Artilleriedivision.

The regiments of the field and mountain artillery each consisted of two 'divisions' of two or three batteries each. Field artillery gun and howitzer batteries had six pieces; horse, mountain and heavy field howitzer batteries had only four pieces. The fortress artillery formed regiments of two or three battalions, and independent battalions, each of them divided into four companies with two to six pieces each.

As a special weapon the k.u.k. Heer also employed **armoured trains** on most fronts. Most of these were built by the Hungarian MAV (State Railways) and armed with naval guns removed

Tyrolean Standschützen home defence volunteers, all in middle age or older, guarding a fortress on the Italian border. Under magnification their grass-green collar patches show the distinctive Tyrolean eagle badge specially granted to these units. The left hand man wears the pike-grey uniform; the others have been issued the darker 1915 field-grey jacket with stand-and-fall collar. At the beginning of the war some men wore only brassards, in the Tyrolean colours of green over white. (Kriegsarchiv)

from disarmed warships or obtained directly from the naval arsenal. The crews were mixed and drawn from specialist branches as required. They usually consisted of members of the k.u.k. Eisenbahnregiment (Railway Regiment) together with officers and men from the infantry, artillery and sappers to man the various weapons. While these trains were, of course, of use only along railway tracks, the Austro-Hungarian forces also experimented with home produced armoured cars; these will be discussed in the second book of this series. The **Sappers** were distinct from the regular **Pioneers.** The primary mission of the latter was the building of bridges, but the former developed several specialist units during the war. The first of these was a *Spezialformation* for the 24cm Luftminen-werfer, which operated on several fronts. This was soon followed by the Sappeurspezialbataillon, which was employed to a certain extent in gas warfare; it was later renamed k.u.k. Sappeurbataillon 62. Another special unit was raised to develop the use of flame-throwers, and this later became k.u.k. Sappeurbataillon 61.

Facing colours of technical troops:
Artillery: scarlet, yellow buttons
Sappers: cherry-red, yellow buttons
Pioneers: steel-green, yellow buttons
Railway troops: steel-green, yellow buttons
Telegraph troops: steel-green, yellow buttons
Train (transport) units: light blue, white buttons
Medical troops: madder-red, yellow buttons

Aviation troops did not have a distinctive facing colour and were only identified by adding the balloon emblem behind the rank device on the collar patch.

STANDSCHÜTZEN & VOLUNTEERS

The Standschützen had a particular tradition among the population of the mountainous areas of the Tyrol and Vorarlberg. Deriving from 'rifle associations', they had shown their loyalty to the Habsburgs for centuries. One of their most remarkable episodes was the Tyrolean resistance led by the famous Andreas Hofer in 1809 against Napoleon's allied Bavarian and Saxon troops.

According to the special rights granted to the Tyrol and Vorarlberg, these associations were allowed to bear firearms 'in perpetuo', which meant that everyone belonging to one of the associations (which were organised for practical purposes in towns, villages or valley communities) kept his rifle at home. When general mobilisation took the able-bodied age classes for the Army, the older men and boys left behind had to form the main strength of these clubs. As a special

Many Standschützen saw active field service in punishing terrain and weather; being of strong mountain farmer stock rather than townsmen, they gave a good account of themselves, despite being recruited from schoolboys and grandfathers. Both ends of the age range are represented in this group from Kastelruth and southern Tyrol photographed in a high mountain position. Their uniforms and equipment are a motley selection; note that most wearing 'snow shirts' with hoods or matching cap covers. (Kriegsarchiv)

tradition they usually elected their 'officers' and 'NCOs' by democratic vote.

In 1915, when Italy threatened the Tyrol once again, the associations showed their loyalty by offering to perform home defence duties; the offer was welcomed, and within a short time numbers variously estimated at between 20,000 and 24,000 were under arms, ranging from schoolboys to grandfathers whose military experience was decades in the past. Interestingly, the 'Welschtiroler' (southern Tyrolese whose mother tongue was Italian) joined in considerable strength – some 3,500 – and remained loyal.

In spring 1915 the equipment of the Standschützen was rather poor, some being identified only by a brassard. During the months which followed it improved considerably; they were supplied with field-grey loden uniforms and, eventually, M95 Mannlicher rifles. As a distinction, their collar patches bore the Tyrolean eagle or the arms of Vorarlberg behind the rank device. Since their officers were not really trained the bureaucracy decided to give them rosettes as rank insignia instead of regular officers' stars; photographs show that this regulation was widely disobeyed, with both officers and NCOs wearing regular stars on their patches. Officers who carried sabres were to fix a silver woven portépée (fist strap) instead of the regular officers' gold equivalent.

On campaign the Standschützen formed companies and – in cases of more than 200 men coming forward from the same region – battalions. They developed remarkable fighting abilities in the defence of the line high in the mountains, but they were naturally unsuitable for mobile campaigning. Furthermore, as the younger men reached military age and some of the older ones became less fit, there was a natural dwindling in numbers, to about half the original figure by May 1917.

Patriotic sentiment, especially after the declaration of war by Italy, favoured the formation of **volunteer 'rifle' units** among the Austrian population, partly on the same basis as the Standschützen organisation in the Tyrol and Vorarlberg.

Thus, a number of units from battalion to sometimes regimental strength were formed: in Carinthia (Kärntner Freiwillige Schützen), Upper Austria (Oberösterreichische Freiwillige Schützen), Salzburg (k.k. freiwillige Schützen Salzburgs), Styria (Steirisches freiwilliges

Schützenbataillon), Vienna (Wiener Bürger Scharfschützenkorps), Marburg (k.k. freiwilliges Schützenbataillon Marburg No.IV), Laibach (k.k. freiwilliges Schützenbataillon Laibach No.V, and the cyclists of the k.k. freiwilliges Schützenbataillon No.201), and Trieste (k.u.k. freiwilliges Schützenbataillon Triest No.VII).

The equipment of these units varied a great deal, from Mannlicher rifles of all models to 'Mexican' Mausers and even Russian M91 Mosin-Nagants. Many wore uniforms based on pike-grey of varying shades (like the 'Mohrengrau' of the Carinthians); but stocks were quickly exhausted, and these were soon replaced by field-grey regulation issue items in all possible combinations. As Schützen their facing colour was Rifle grass-green bearing the arms of the battalion's region behind the rank device. Again, they were ordered to wear rosettes instead of rank stars, but as soon as these units reached the front these were in many cases hastily replaced by stars so that their wearers would not be considered as 'irregulars' by the enemy. Some of the units, like the k.k. Kärntner freiwilliges Schützenregiment, were granted the stars officially at a later date. Elected officers were ordered to have silver portépées, but those coming from the Army or Landwehr organisation were entitled to gold.

FOREIGN VOLUNTEERS

Political activities at the time of the outbreak of the Great War favoured the existence of nationalist clubs and associations, sometimes not only of political agitators but also organised as 'rifle associations' vaguely comparable to the Tyrolean Standschützen. Their peacetime sporting activities became extremely politicised when the international situation deteriorated towards military conflict. Despite the long confrontation – some would claim, an underground war – between the Austro-Hungarian authorities and the various clandestine nationalist groups which sought the break-up of the Empire, the government was not above using such groups when they threatened Austro-Hungary's enemies.

A platoon of infantrymen from the Polish Legion, some (e.g. left foreground) wearing the *maciejowka* cap. Their uniform items and equipment show a considerable variety of origin and date. (Kriegsarchiv)

The Polish Legion

Most prominent among the foreign volunteers were the Poles, fighting for the cause of an independent and united nation of Poland. The third division of Poland in 1795 had been ratified at the Congress of Vienna in 1815: Austria received West Galicia, with its capital Krakow, and Eastern Galicia with its capital at Lemberg (Lvov); Prussia (after 1871, the German Empire) got West Prussia and Posen (Poznan). The remainder –

Members of a Ulan squadron of the Polish Legion at Alt-Sandec. Left and right, note the distinctive high cap based on the traditional *czapka;* the central man wears a peakless field cap with a squared crown, reminiscent of the old *confederatka.* All three wear fleece-collared *Pelzulanka* jackets based on the Austro-Hungarian design, and are armed with the M04 Austro-Hungarian cavalry sabre. (Kriegsarchiv)

nearly 80 per cent of the former Polish nation with perhaps 60 per cent of the population – passed into Russian hands. After 1867 the Austro-Hungarian authorities favoured the Galician provinces by granting a certain degree of internal autonomy and freedom of cultural activities, thus making the Dual Monarchy comparatively attractive for the rest of Poland.

The main objective for Polish activities remained either a unification of all Polish regions to form an autonomous area within the Russian Empire, or – more radically – the restoration of an independent Polish state.

Joséf Pilsudski, later the president of independent Poland, became the commander of the unified *strzelcy* ('riflemen') movement on 30 July 1914. On 19 August 1914 the AOK agreed to the formation in East and West Galicia of a Polish Legion, officially permitted to use the Polish language, and Pilsudski became the commander of its 1st Regiment. Despite the critical strategic situation the Legion attracted so many volunteers that this unit had to be expanded into the 1st Polish Legion Brigade in November 1914. It suffered heavily during the winter campaign of 1914/15, but continued to attract so many recruits that after a priod of rest in early spring it was able to go back into the line between March and July 1915.

With Lemberg occupied by the Russians, in late 1914 a 2nd Polish Legion was formed from East Galician volunteers in Krakow, with two regiments of infantry, three batteries of field artillery and two cavalry squadrons. It fought with distinction in the hard Carpathian winter and in 1915 was active in the Bukovina and Bessarabia. Later a smaller 3rd Brigade was formed. All three brigades were used to halt the Brusilov Offensives, and were re-organised into a *Polnisches Hilfskorps* ('Polish Auxiliary Corps') in August 1916.

In 1917 the attempted re-creation of a Kingdom of Poland failed, causing political problems that were further aggravated by the First Revolution in Russia. At around this time the Legion was disbanded, with only elements of the 2nd Brigade remaining loyal until early 1918.

The uniforms of the Polish units varied enormously and photographs show a perturbing variety of garments, uniform designs and rank distinctions. However, some main items may be noted. Headgear was either the Polish soft cap with a Prussian peak, the *maciejowka*, or the distinctive *rogatywka* with its square crown. The Ulans of the cavalry squadrons favoured the high czakpa recalling the Napoleonic period, but a slightly lower and smaller version could also be seen. In all cases a variety of cockades and shields were applied, mostly showing the Polish eagle with inscriptions e.g. 'S' for *strzelcy* or 'L' for *legiony*. Rank badges consisted of bars for NCOs, and for officers stars in combination with the distinctive Polish 'zig-zag' lace, in 1914–16 in red for subalterns and silver for staff officers. As with the Tyrolean and Austrian volunteers, the rank devices were ordered to be rosettes rather than stars, causing irritation among the legionaries; some even discarded their rank badges in protest. Later, in 1916, following new regulations, the red 'zig-zag' lace passed to the NCOs, officers receiving silver or (for staff officers) gold lace in combination with stars.

Generally, pike-grey cloth was issued for the uniforms, and the jackets were tailored with a touch of the Polish cut; trousers were worn with woollen stockings or puttees. Later the colour became field-grey, mostly in the same cut. A great variety of detail differences can be seen in surviving photographs, including Polish legionaries dressed in full Austro-Hungarian regulation uniforms. Photographs also show that even within single units headgear and clothing varied to a certain extent.

While the 1st Legion Brigade's infantry collar patches varied from red to none, the 2nd Legion Brigade seems to have had green patches throughout. In other units carmine red has been reported for Ulans, black for artillery and white for the medical service. Weapons included either Austro-Hungarian standard issue of all available models for the infantry, with the M04 cavalry sabre for the Ulans, although the latter also used former Russian cavalry sabres. Officers were usually issued the M61 Austrian infantry officer's sabre worn from the *Kuppel* underneath the jacket, with silver/red striped portépées, but photographs also show infantry officers carrying Russian infantry sabres.

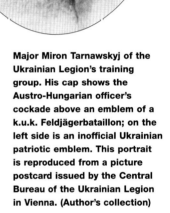

Major Miron Tarnawskyj of the Ukrainian Legion's training group. His cap shows the Austro-Hungarian officer's cockade above an emblem of a k.u.k. Feldjägerbataillon; on the left side is an inofficial Ukrainian patriotic emblem. This portrait is reproduced from a picture postcard issued by the Central Bureau of the Ukrainian Legion in Vienna. (Author's collection)

The Ukrainian Legion

Following practically the same agenda as the Polish Legion, Ukrainian (Ruthenian) separatists volunteered to fight for an independent state of 'Ukraina'. Ukrainian political groups supported the formation of a regiment of two battalions totalling 2,500 men, incorporated in the Austro-Hungarian Army's XXV Korps. At first named 'Ukrainian Rifle Volunteers' (freiwillige ukrainische Schützen), they later received the title Ukrainische Legion; the word 'Legion-' was always used before the officers' rank titles.

From 1914 to 1916 they wore Austro-Hungarian uniforms of pike-grey and later field-grey, with light blue collar patches with a narrow yellow stripe at the rear edge – the Ukrainian colours. Rank distinctions included stars which were arranged in a horizontal line along the collar patch.

Towards the turn of 1916/17 the collar patch was reduced to a small light blue/yellow stripe; and a new headgear was designed, which was

Gallipoli, winter 1915/16: men of k.u.k. Motor-Mörserbatterie No.9 posing with their Turkish allies. The Austrians are wearing field-grey overcoats. See Plate H1. (Kriegsarchiv)

introduced during 1917. In 1918 most elements of this Legion formed the cadre of the new independent Ukrainian army.

Most unusually, they were also allowed to have women in their ranks; some of them were even decorated for bravery during the war.

The Albanian Legion

In spring 1916 the k.u.k. XIX Korps, which had entered the northern and central parts of Albania, began to reorganise the internal security system of that country. Elements from the Austrian k.k. Gendarmerie helped to organise and train Albanian gendarmerie units and set up police units in towns such as Tirana and Elbassan.

Distinct from this police force, the Army tried to establish a new military system by forming Albanian militias on a territorial basis. Nine battalions each of four companies of 150 to 175 men were formed in the course of 1916, and remained active until 1918. Officers and NCOs came from the Austro-Hungarian Army. In some cases certain tribes volunteered collectively with their chiefs. Usually the Albanians wore Austro-Hungarian regular uniforms of field-grey material with distinctive headgear, which could be either the Albanian white conical fez or a grey cylindrical fez displaying a cockade in the red/black national colours. There is also evidence that some volunteers continued to wear their national costumes.

These *Albanerbataillone* served within their country alongside the Austro-Hungarian forces against Italians, French and Greeks until 1918. In 1917 special clothing instructions were proposed, but as far as is known these were never issued. Arms and equipment included both standard Austro-Hungarian issue and various kinds of captured weapons.

AUSTRO-HUNGARIAN UNITS ON TURKISH FRONTS

During the fight for the Gallipoli Peninsula the Turkish war minister, Enver Pasha, asked for support for the hard-pressed defenders. During the primary stages of the campaign no direct support was possible because Serbia blocked the route down the Balkans. In autumn 1915 an Austro-Hungarian/German force under the command of Generalfeld-marshall von Mackensen defeated the Serbian army and opened the way for direct support to Turkey. In December 1915 two Austro-Hungarian artillery units were transported down the River Danube and finally reached Gallipoli. The 15cm Haubitzbatterie No.36 reached the Sogan lidere opposite Sedd-ul bar, and the 24cm Motormörserbatterie

No.9 took position around Anafarta, shelling ANZAC troops from there. Both units took part in the final stages of this campaign.

In 1916 the 15cm Haubitzbatterie No.36 moved to the Smyrna area for coastal defence duties; here its gunfire sank the British Monitor M30. The 24cm Motormörserbatterie was divided in 1916: two guns were sent for coastal defence to Mount Carmel near Haifa in Palestine, where they remained. The other half of the battery was re-equipped with new 10.4cm guns and named 10cm Kanonenbatterie No.20; it saw action in the second and third battles of Gaza, and the two battles of the Jordan valley.

In 1916 a mountain howitzer division ('Gebirgshaubitzdivision von Marno'), consisting of two batteries of 10cm mountain howitzers, joined the second Turkish attempt to win control over the Suez Canal. The division at first attacked during the battle of Romani, but suddenly found itself in a rearguard position when the Turkish front line collapsed. Astonishingly, the Austro-Hungarian unit proved equal to the situation, and succeeded in bringing all their pieces back to a new defence line on the fringe of the Negev Desert.

The division remained in the area; in 1917 it was renamed 'k.u.k. Gebirgshaubitzdivision in der Türkei'. Finally, re- equipped with field howitzers in early 1918, it was again renamed 'k.u.k. Feldhaubitz-abteilung in der Türkei'. It fought with distinction in all three battles of Gaza, covered the Turkish retreat, fought in both battles of the Jordan valley, and finally marched in the direction of Aleppo.

Apart from these combat units, the Austro-Hungarian Army sent nearly a dozen instruction detachments to train the Turkish artillery in the use of Skoda mountain guns and howitzers. Ski training was also given to Turkish mountain soldiers. Particularly effective were medical institutions such as a field hospital in Jerusalem, a field ambulance at Bir-Sebba, and two mobile field hospitals which joined in 1917. During the final retreat one of the latter, the k.u.k. Feldspital No.309, was completely destroyed by an Australian air raid. At least four lorry transport columns (k.u.k. Auto-kolonnen Türkei Nos.1- 4) supported the Turks between Diarbekhir and Mosul.

During all these operations the Austro-Hungarian units always operated in support to the Ottoman forces and, in contrast to military elements from Germany, they never passed under Ottoman administrative control. In 1918 the survivors were concentrated in Haidar Pasha (Constantinople); they were repatriated via Trieste in early 1919.

Firing position of a 24cm mortar of k.u.k. Motor-Mörserbatterie No.9 at Anafarta, Gallipoli, in 1915/16.
The soldiers wear pike-grey jackets with field-grey trousers and puttees. (Kriegsarchiv)

THE PLATES

A1: *Hauptmann, k.u.k. Infanterieregiment No.4 'Hoch- und Deutschmeister'*, summer 1914

This captain of a Vienna regiment offers a vivid example of an Austro-Hungarian officer during the very early stages of the war, wearing the traditional officer's sash, the field sign on his cap, and riding boots. As a captain he would be mounted and in command of a company. He is equipped with an M07 Repetierpistole, and the M61 sabre with gold lace portépée hangs from the *Kuppel*, a belt usually worn underneath the jacket. His decoration bar shows the 1898 Jubilee Medal and the Jubilee Cross of 1908.

A2: *Hauptmann im Generalstabskorps*, summer 1914

Generals and officers of the General Staff were identified by their distinctive high, stiff képi-style caps with a gold lace cockade and loop. Other details include the red-edged, black silk collar patch of the General Staff. Captain was the lowest rank in the Generalstabskorps. He wears the officer's sash over his waistbelt, and is armed with a 7.65mm Steyr Kipplauf pistol. Typical ribbons would be the Jubilee Medal of 1898, the Jubilee Cross of 1908, and the Mobilisation Cross of 1912/13.

A3: *Oberleutnant der Artillerie*

The most distinctive features of this artillery first lieutenant's uniform are the *Kartuscheriemen* (cartridge pouch belt) across the chest, and the *Achseldragoner* made of gold/black striped lace on his left shoulder. He is armed with the M04 cavalry sabre with gold fist strap, and an M98 Rast & Gasser revolver. Note his gaiters.

B1: *Korporal, k.u.k. Infanterieregiment No.27 'Albert I, König der Belgier'*, summer 1914

This corporal represents the standard type of Austro-Hungarian infantry from 'German' regiments at the outbreak of war; his unit was raised in the Graz region of Styria in Austria. He wears the 1908 field uniform with *Hosenspangen* (small gaiters) and full equipment, and is armed with the M95 Mannlicher rifle. On the left side of his cap he displays the field sign of an oakleaf, typical for the first few weeks of the war only. Note the *Schützenauszeichnung* (marksmanship lanyard, 2nd Class) on his left shoulder; and the proficiency badge for *Distanzschätzung* (distance judging) on his right breast.

B2: *Zugsführer, k.u.k. Infanterieregiment No.53 'General Dankl'*

This sergeant represents the 'Hungarian' component of the Common Army, wearing the light summer field jacket with stand-and-fall collar. He belongs to a Croatian regiment raised in the Agram/Zagreb area; Croatian units were incorporated in the Hungarian half of the Dual Monarchy and dressed like Hungarian regiments with their distinctive trousers. He is armed with the standard M95 Mannlicher; note on his left shoulder the 1st Class marksman's lanyard.

B3: *Feldwebel, k.u.k bosnisch-herzegowinisches Infanterieregiment No.4*

This staff sergeant serves with a regiment raised in the Mostar region. The fez was the most distinctive item worn by the Bosnian-Herzegovinian regiments, which soon earned a high reputation for bravery and loyalty. The colour of the fez was changed from red to pike-grey for field

The swansong of the old imperial and royal cavalry: two Dragoon trumpeters – a Zugsführer (sergeant) and a Korporal – in their field uniforms at the outbreak of war. They carry the lambswool–lined overjacket slung like a pelisse; the tunic is pale blue with regimental facings at collar and cuffs, the breeches red. On campaign their helmets were either covered with grey cloth or simply overpainted grey. See Plate C. (Kriegsarchiv)

uniforms. He is armed with an M07 Repetierpistole and, in keeping with his rank, with a sabre furnished with a black/yellow wool fist strap.

B4: *Tambour, k.u.k. Infanterieregiment No.97 'Freiherr von Waldstätten'*

This drummer from a Trieste regiment is armed with the M53/62 Pioneer sword; nevertheless, the red wool lanyard indicates his qualification as a marksman. The drums were usually produced from polished aluminium and were hastily overpainted pike-grey for low visibility in the field. By the end of September 1914 drums were removed from the troops and the former drummers served on as normal infantrymen.

C1: *Korporal, k.u.k. Dragonerregiment No.10 'Fürst von Liechtenstein'*

Dragoons were identified by their facing colours and differently coloured buttons. As a corporal he is armed with an M07 Repetierpistole and the M04 cavalry sabre. His distinctive dragoon helmet, in peacetime shining black with brass fittings, has been overpainted grey in a gesture towards the needs of a field uniform.

C2: *Ulan, k.u.k. Ulanenregiment No.2 'Fürst zu Schwarzenberg'*

Against cold weather this trooper is wearing the *Pelzulanka*

Korporal (left) and Schütze of Tiroler Landesschützen ('Tyrolean Territorial Rifles'), armed with M95 carbines and issued with both climbing equipment – long ice pick and rope – and skis, with one stick only. They display the Edelweiss on their grass-green collar patches, and the blackcock feather on the left side of their caps; cf Plates E1 & E2. (Kriegsarchiv)

RIGHT A posed portrait of an elderly Standschütze home defence volunteer wearing the field-grey loden jacket issued from late 1915; see Plate E4. No collar patches are worn here. Note the appearance of the breast pockets; the Austrian double eagle buckle plate (this was replaced by the Hungarian coat of arms in Hungarian units); the national cockade on the front of the cap crown, pierced with the imperial/royal monogram 'FJI'; and the typical addition of non-regulation badges to the left side of the field cap. (Kriegsarchiv)

with its black lambskin collar. His *czapka* lance cap has a grey linen cover; the horsehair plumes were sometimes removed, but not always. He is armed with the M95 carbine, and the M04 cavalry sabre with a red leather *Faustriemen* fist strap.

C3: *Wachtmeister, k.u.k. Husarenregiment No.13 'Friedrich Wilhelm Kronprinz des Deutschen Reiches und Kronprinz von Preussen'*

This long service NCO in his early forties wears the Attila, decorated with the well-known Hungarian knot *(vitez-kötes)* on the sleeve and oval 'olive' buttons. The trousers are also of typical Hungarian cut, as are the *czismen* boots of black leather. The sleeve bears the long-service chevrons of yellow ribbon, and his decorations are the *Militärdienstzeichen* (long service decoration), the Jubilee

Medal of 1898, the Jubilee Cross of 1908, and the 1912/13 Mobilisation Cross. The only item of field equipment is the grey linen shako cover.

C4: *Zugsführer-Trompeter, k.u. Honvéd Husarenregiment No.4*

This sergeant-trumpeter serves with a unit recruited in the Szegedin area. He wears the red cavalry undress peakless forage cap with brass other ranks' cockade pierced with the royal cypher in Hungarian style – '1FJ'. On the side – hidden here – a brass regimental number was usually pinned. The trumpet cord is in the traditional Honvéd colour of cherry-red.

D1: Austrian *Landsturmmann*, autumn/winter 1914/15

This figure represents a soldier of the Austrian k.k. Landsturm, issued with the pre-1908 blue uniform due to shortages of pike-grey field dress at the beginning of the war. The *paroli* (facing colour patches) have been removed from the dark blue-grey overcoat. He is armed with the M88/90 Mannlicher rifle (the first to take smokeless powder cartridges), and has the old pre-1908 black leather issue field equipment with large ammunition pouches.

D2: General Staff officer, improvised winter uniform; Carpathian Mountains, winter 1914/15

A General Staff officer on campaign protects himself against the winter cold with two greatcoats. The outer one shows the distinctive *paroli* in black silk piped with red, and he wears an officer's waistbelt, lanyard and sidearm over the inner coat.

D3: Infantryman in marching order, winter 1914/15

This typical soldier is taken from a photograph showing the arrival of a column of reinforcements in the front lines in

K.k. Gendarmerie of the railway station security detachment at Tarvis, Carinthia, wearing khaki-covered cork helmets with brass fittings; see Plate F2. This photograph was posed to show uniform details; when on duty as Military Police (Feldgendarmerie) they would wear a yellow/black/yellow brassard with the inscription 'Feldgendarm'. (Kriegsarchiv)

the Carpathians. He has his greatcoat collar turned up, and is armed with the standard Mannlicher M95 rifle.

E1: Korporal, k.k. Landwehrinfanterieregiment No.4 Klagenfurt, spring 1915

A corporal of the Austrian Landwehr with *Alpinausrüstung* mountain climbing gear; his regiment was one of those specially trained and equipped for mountain warfare. The uniform, of rather 'sporting' cut, was introduced from 1907 at first for the Tyrolean Landesschützen and later for the other mountain units of the k.k. Landwehr. Distinctive items were the blackcock feather worn on the cap, and the white metal Edelweiss badge behind the rank device on the 'grass-green' collar patches. His special equipment includes goggles, heavy boots, ropes, an ice pick, and the M95 Mannlicher Repetierstutzen carbine.

E2: Tyrolean Landesschütze with ski equipment

In severe weather this mountain soldier wears the overcoat influenced by Alpine sports clothing, cut generously loose with an expanding rear pleat so as to protect both the man and his equipment. Note the shape of the skis; either one or two sticks might be used.

E3: Schütze, Kärntner Freiwillige Schützen, autumn 1916

This Carinthian Volunteer Rifleman is a youngster, perhaps from the final class of secondary school. The uniform shown is the 1916 issue in field-grey with a stand-and-fall collar, and grass-green patches showing the emblem of the Kärntner Freiwillige Schützen. He is armed with

a 7mm Mauser Infanteriegewehr M14 (the famous 'Mexican' Mauser).

E4: Tyrolean Standschütze, south Tyrolean front, autumn 1915/spring 1916

This type of proper uniform was received from autumn 1915 together with other items of regulation Army equipment and weapons. Before that date the volunteers were issued anything that was available from depots in the Tyrol, and considerable numbers wore civilain clothing with only a brassard to indicate their military status. The collar patches of grass-green bore the Tyrolean eagle or the arms of Vorarlberg in white metal behind any rank device. In many cases these were hardly visible behind the mighty beards which were popular in the Tyrol. This Standschütze serving in the Dolomites is armed with the standard M95 Mannlicher.

F1: Sapper, Isonzo front, early 1916

A typical example of weather improvisations; he wears the standard early pike-grey field tunic with later field-grey trousers tucked into jackboots of the Pioneer type; a privately acquired pullover worn under the jacket is folded outwards, covering the upper collar as well as helping to ward off the cold dampness of the Isonzo (Soca) valley. The natural brown waistbelt is the M15 type, with M95 bayonet attached.

F2: Austrian Feldgendarm, Isonzo front, 1915/16

The Gendarmerie belonged to the k.k. Landwehr organisation and elements were mobilised to form the military police in the field. This Gendarm wears a greatcoat, and the typical khaki cloth-covered cork helmet with brass fittings; later the standard field cap would steadily replace this headgear. He is armed with the M90 Gendarmerie rifle with bayonet and the M51 Gendarmerie sabre. The brassard indicates his status as a *Feldgendarm*, i.e. a military policeman.

F3: Officer, Royal Hungarian Gendarmerie (Mounted), winter 1915/16

The Hungarian Gendarmerie wore black hats with brass badges and cock feathers instead of the spiked helmets of the Austrians. This officer's Dragoon-type *Pelzrock* overcoat of field-grey cloth is worn with matching riding breeches and Hungarian *cismen* riding boots. Equipment includes the M61 officer's sabre with gold fist strap and the M07 Repetierpistole.

F4: Gefreiter, k.k. Landwehrinfanterieregiment No.23; Podgora (Gorizia), spring 1916

This regiment, together with No.37, gained a high reputation for hard fighting along the Isonzo front, especially in the area around Görz (Gorizia). Being Dalmatians they were familiar with the Italian language, and took the Italians by surprise when counter-attacking. For hand-to-hand fighting both armies favoured improvised weapons such as spades and daggers, and both re-invented archaic implements like the spiked trench club carried here. This lance-corporal wears the field-grey tunic with stand-and-fall collar, together with *Kniehose* trousers and *Wadenstutzen* woollen stockings. His main weapon is a slung M95 Repetierstutzen carbine.

G1: Zugskommandant, Polish Legion late 1915

This officer, equivalent to a first lieutenant, is already dressed in field-grey with some 'Polish' alterations to the Austro-Hungarian cut; his cap is the *maciejowka*. His equipment is purely Austro-Hungarian, consisting of the M61 officer's sabre with silver portépée and the M98 Rast & Gasser revolver.

G2: *Ulan*, Polish Legion, mid-1915

This uniform is preserved in the Heeresgeschichtliches Museum (Army Museum) in Vienna. It includes the high *czapka* with brown leather fittings and the Legion's Polish eagle badge. The *Ulanka* field blouse is very similar to Austro-Hungarian Ulan cut, but made of a lighter shade of field-grey cloth and with cherry-red piping round the pocket flaps and down the front; the collar patches are the same colour. He is armed with an M04 Austro-Hungarian cavalry sabre.

G3: Soldier, Polish Legion infantry, late 1914

During the early stages of the Great War the Polish Legion received pike-grey cloth from which the uniforms were tailored in a 'Polish' cut; later issues also saw Polish Legion soldiers wearing full Austro-Hungarian uniforms. Note the distinctive Polish *rogatywka* cap, its square crown recalling the historic shape of the *czapka*. He is armed with the standard M95 Mannlicher and wears regulation leather equipment.

G4: *Legions-Zugskommandant*, Ukrainian Legion, autumn 1916

The Ukrainian volunteers wore standard Austro-Hungarian

The most obvious distinction was the collar patch of light blue with a yellow stripe at the end, and the rank stars arranged in a single line. This first lieutenant is armed with an M98 revolver.

H1: *Kanonier, 24cm Motor-Mörserbatterie No.9*; Anafarta, Gallipoli, Turkey, winter 1915/16

Before leaving for Turkey the Austro-Hungarian artillery contingent were issued the modern field-grey uniform in the best available quality – the winter weather on the Gallipoli peninsula made it necessary. This gunner's waistbelt is of cavalry type with two ammunition pouches.

H2: *Major, 15cm Haubitzbatterie No.36*; Gulf of Saros (Smyrna), spring 1916

Classic khaki tropical uniforms were issued in Constantinople only and consisted of a sun helmet and khaki garments, sometimes of the same cut as the pike-grey equivalents. His equipment is standard. Note the ribbons of the 'Signum Laudis' (Medal of Merit), 1898 Jubilee Medal, 1908 Jubilee Cross and, on the fly front, the German Iron Cross; on the right breast he wears the Turkish Iron Crescent.

H3: *Zugsführer, Gebirgshaubitzdivision von Marno*; Palestine, summer 1916

The cut of the sergeant's khaki tropical blouse is the same as the summer pattern 1908 pike-grey field jacket. His sun helmet has the standard other ranks' cockade (darkened), with the lettering 'FJI'. The waist belt is of cavalry type, and would support the bayonet for the M95 Repetierkarabiner with the NCOs' tassel. On the upper right breast he wears the gunlayer's proficiency badge made of Tombak alloy; he too has the Turkish Iron Crescent decoration, and he displays the German Iron Cross ribbon on the fly front of the tunic.

H4: *Korporal, Autokolonne Türkei No.2*; Diarbekhir, summer/autumn 1916

This corporal driver's khaki tropical jacket still has concealed buttonholes, which indicates that the uniform was tailored in early 1916. His field cap is the standard issue, again made of light khaki material. Khaki trousers and puttees, brown leather belt and bayonet with yellow/black tassel complete his outfit. He displays the bronze Medal for Bravery on its white/red ribbon. Both H3 and H4 display a facing colour stripe on the collar in place of the old patches.

Palestine, 1916: camp scene of k.u.k. Gebirgshaubitzdivision von Marno. Officers and men are dressed in khaki tropical uniforms; the usual national cockade is fixed to the front of the sun helmets. The sabre was not carried in the field. See Plate H2. (Kriegsarchiv)

RIGHT Camp of k.u.k. Autokolonne Türkei No.2 at Diarbekhir, late 1916; see Plate H4. The sun helmets worn with the khaki tropical uniforms do not bear the national cockade. The lorries are 3-ton Fiat *'Subventions Lastwagen'*. (Kriegsarchiv)

INDEX